BEYOND THE GULF WAR
The Middle East and the New World Order

edited by John Gittings

BEYOND THE GULF WAR
The Middle East and the New World Order

edited by John Gittings

CIIR
in association with
The Gulf Conference Committee

First published 1991

Catholic Institute for International Relations, Unit 3, Canonbury Yard, 190a New North Road, London N1 7BJ in association with the Gulf Conference Committee, London.

© CIIR 1991

British Library Cataloguing in Publication Data
Beyond the Gulf War: The Middle East and the New World Order
    I. Gittings, John, 1938-
    327.0917671

    ISBN 1 85287 083 4

Cover and text design by Rich Cowley
Cover photo: Kurdish refugees at Isikveren camp straddling Turkey/Iraq border (Roger Hutchings/Katz Pictures)

Printed in the UK by Russell Press Ltd., Nottingham

Contents

Acknowledgements	vii
An Iraqi appeal	viii
Introduction John Gittings	1

1 A NEW WORLD ORDER?

How the West mobilised for war Richard Falk	12
From the cauldron of war to the chaos of peace Alain Gresh	23
Western celebration and Arab outrage Fadia Faqir	31

2 ARAB STATES AND IDEOLOGIES

The Arab regional system and the Gulf crisis Yezid Sayigh	38
Racism and Islam Haleh Afshar	46
The Arab world and the need for cultural renewal Khalil Hindi	54
Ba'athist power and the future of Saddam Marion Farouk-Sluglett and Peter Sluglett	60

3 THE UNJUST WAR

Counting the costs of a 'simple war' Michael Gilsenan	68
Arab losses, First World gains Tim Niblock	77
The United States and Palestine: Avoiding the issue Abbas Shiblak	86
Syria and Egypt and the spoils of war Youssef Choueiri	92

4 A BLIGHTED FUTURE
An experiment in the unknown
Fred Pearce   96

The post-war Arab world: Development in reverse
Rami Zreik   102

Conclusion
John Gittings   110

APPENDICES
Chronology of the Gulf War   115

Arming Saddam: The supply of British military equipment to Iraq 1979-90 126

The economic impact of the Gulf crisis on Third World countries   133

The Palestinian memo to James Baker   138

Contributors   141

Acknowledgements

This book is based upon the proceedings of a conference held in London on 9 March 1991 on the theme 'Beyond the Gulf War'. The conference was organised by the Gulf Conference Committee on behalf of Media Workers Against the War. The MWAW had convened at the start of the Gulf War, bringing together hundreds of journalists and other media workers who were deeply concerned both by the implications of the war and by the manipulation of news about it. Some material in this book was first presented at the Catholic Institute for International Relations, which held its own conference on the Middle East on 17 April. Part of the paper by Michael Gilsenan is based on his essay in *Marxism Today*, March 1991. Part of Alain Gresh's paper is based on his article in *Le Monde Diplomatique*, February 1991. The paper by Fred Pearce was specially commissioned for this book. The Committee thanks its supporters whose financial help, promptly given, made the original conference possible, and all the contributors, who gave their services free of charge. We also gratefully acknowledge the assistance of the CIIR and of the Joseph Rowntree Charitable Trust in subsidising this publication.

Special thanks go to Judith Booth, secretary of the GCC, who has tackled so many of the editing chores needed to produce this book. We acknowledge the initiative of Victoria Brittain, without whom the original conference would not have taken place. The chronology was produced by Don Redding. We also thank Jane Gough for her translation of Alain Gresh's article and Jan Parker, Nick Richmond and Noll Scott for their technical help. We are grateful too for the hard work of CIIR's publications section and other staff.

Gulf Conference Committee
May 1991

An Iraqi appeal

We Iraqi artists and writers who were forced to leave our homeland because of repression and war believe that Saddam Hussein's ill-adventure in Kuwait could have been resolved by peaceful means within the Arab and international framework. The continuation of the war in spite of Iraq's withdrawal indicates the existence of another American resolution unrelated to the United Nations resolutions. In the name of liberating Kuwait they are destroying Iraq with all its human, cultural, economic and military resources and increasing its economic and military dependence. That Hussein agreed to negotiate a withdrawal before the ground war was initiated by the US confirms this hidden agenda.

The Iraqi nation has suffered many wars. Besides the war with Iran, Saddam Hussein has waged an undeclared war against the Iraqi people particularly in the Kurdish area. Yet Hussein continued to be supported and pampered by the capitalist West and by the socialist East and enjoyed the sympathies of the rich Gulf kingdoms.

Today with the scene reversed the victim remains the Iraqi people. Iraq has been caught between the flames ignited by the allies and those of an unmerciful oppressor.

We have stopped our songs and verses because of the tragedy which has befallen our land, the cradle of civilisation and the birthplace of the first alphabet and human laws. We beseech the hearts and conscience of the world to stand alongside us in this very dark hour. We call upon you to stand against any attempts to substitute Saddam Hussein with another oppressor or with an imported government forced upon a reluctant nation. We call upon you to stand up against any attempts to burden Iraq with the costs of a war it had no will to fight.

We appeal to the heart and conscience of the international community to offer economic and medical aid that will be needed by a nation seeking peace and freedom.

Suad Al-Jazairi (journalist)
Sadik Al-Saygh (poet)
Sharif Al-Robbaii (poet)
Hashim Shafik (poet)
Roonak Shouki (theatre director)
Zuheir Al-Jazzairi (writer)

Aziz Al-Naib (calligrapher)
Falah Hashim (actor)
Kadim Khalifa (painter)
Diaa Al-Azzawi (painter)
Sadik Toma (painter)
Kuteiba Al-Janabi (cameraman)

Fauzi Karim (poet)
Ahmed Al-Mohhana (writer)
Faik Batti (journalist)
Fattima Al-Mohsin (writer)
Kasim M Galli (journalist)
Sabbah Al-Shahir (novelist)
Saadi Ahdullatif (writer)
Abdalhusain Shabban (writer)

Abdulla Sikhi (writer)
Jamal Haider (journalist)
Falih Abdul Jabbar (writer)
Karim Gassid (poet)
Raad Moshatat (poet)
Aziz Al-Simawi (poet)
Ali Kamil (cinema director)
Yousif Al-Nassir (painter)

London
9 March 1991

Introduction

John Gittings

This is a book for those who do not believe that the Gulf crisis began on 2 August 1990 and ended on 28 February 1991. To think otherwise is to confront immediately the dominant Western view of this catastrophe — that the crisis arose solely out of Saddam Hussein's aggression against Kuwait, that it could only be resolved by international force of arms, and that the war was a resounding success. This unhistorical view suits the purposes of the victors, who seek to present their previous support for Saddam as irrelevant, and the appalling consequences of the conflict — particularly the agony of the Kurdish people — as essentially unrelated to their conduct of the war

This view also reflects the paradox of modern high-tech news gathering. Instant access is followed by instant oblivion. The occasional blip of grim truth — the bombing of the civilian Amariya shelter in Baghdad, the turkey shoot against the fleeing Iraqi army from Kuwait — soon fades. The video images barely persist long enough to imprint themselves on public consciousness: they leave an impression of a war which lasted 'only 100 hours'. Yet even to say that the 'ground war' was over in four days is a cruel evasion of the truth. Where did the allied bombs fall during the previous 40 days of 'air war' if not on the ground?

Nor did the crisis only last seven months. The Gulf has been in crisis at least since the earlier Gulf War between Iran and Iraq which began in 1980 with covert Western support for the aggressor — Iraq. And the crisis is far from over. It is a continuing crisis which is inextricably linked, as our contributors will show, with long-standing social and political conflict in the Middle East: the backward state system of the Arab countries of which Saddam Hussein is a typical product, the background of chronic tension which the denial of Palestinian rights has provided for decades, and the persistent colonial and post-colonial manipulation of the region by outside powers.

This book emerged from a conference organised in London during the Gulf War by a group of journalists and other media workers on 9 March 1991. Professionally we were deeply disturbed by the news restrictions imposed on our colleagues in the field, and by the distortions, half-truths and lies which found their way into so much comment and analysis. As members of a society which had gone to war, we were distressed by the way in which ideals such as the defence of freedom, support for democracy, and commitment to the United Nations (UN), were being manipulated for a conflict which was fought for different ends. We were also dismayed that the opinions and expertise of scholars and writers from the Middle East, and of many of their specialist colleagues in Britain, were largely excluded from the debate. Though far more profound than those of any television general or sand-pit commentator, they were rarely heard except for the occasional late showing well after midnight.

Principles and politics
The moral discrepancy between stated principles and real politics was even more glaring after the war. For a brief period the conflict was presented (like so many previous wars) as an act of catharsis which should and would lead to higher standards of behaviour in international affairs and particularly in the region. As the bombs were still falling the British Foreign Secretary, Douglas Hurd, in a speech on 2 February at Blaby, put it in the following terms:

> The liberation of Kuwait is a just cause. The people of that little country have suffered grievously from Iraq's aggression. But the coming battle is about more even than that. It is about the sort of world in which we wish to live. In the late 20th century nations must be able to conduct affairs by a code more worthy of rational human beings than the law of the jungle...

In their first glow of victory the makers of war offered themselves to the world as the architects of peace. 'We went half way round the world to do what is moral and just and right,' claimed President Bush on 6 March. His Secretary of State, James Baker, left for the Middle East to capitalise on what he described as 'a honeymoon, a window of opportunity... to look for new formulas to settle old disputes.'[1] Mr Baker was portrayed as an impartial arbitrator doing his best to promote 'new thinking' in the region, as if his own government were an entirely neutral party and not partisan. The allied victors promised peace and security in the region, a determined effort to limit the spread of arms, a new spirit of democracy, and relief — as soon as a ceasefire had been concluded — for the people of Iraq with whom, it was repeatedly stated, they had 'no quarrel'.

But the allied triumph turned to ashes in less than a month, as fleeing Kurds stumbled in northern Iraq over mountain passes towards the Turkish and Iranian borders, while desperate refugees begged for aid from US army posts in the south. It was only too evident that the Kurdish and Shi'a revolts would never have occurred if the Baghdad regime had not been crippled by the war and if the Iraqi people had not been explicitly urged by Mr Bush on 15 February to 'take matters into their own hands and force Saddam Hussein...to step aside'.

The truth of the matter only emerged after the war, when US officials spoke candidly though always anonymously. It was the Iraqi military, not the Iraqi people, they wished to see succeed. They feared that successful rebellions might lead to real self-determination for the people of Iraq — 'a can of worms that no one wants to touch'.[2] Yet the rebellions still had a place in a cynical Western scenario. This envisaged Saddam Hussein being so weakened that the right sort of successor regime — 'the military establishment and other elites' — could then emerge in Iraq.

New 'apples' to sell

Hopes of any slackening in the rush to sell arms to the Middle East are also a mirage in the post-war desert. Mr Bush said after the war that it would be 'tragic' if a new arms race developed; Mr Baker judged that the pre-war arms build-up had been 'absurd'. But administration officials quickly explained that Washington was 'determined to build up the arsenals of friendly Arab states'. Early in March Congress was sent a 'wish-list' for US$18 billion of new arms sales to four Arab allies — Saudi Arabia, the United Arab Emirates, Bahrain, Egypt — and Turkey. US officials were irritated by the idea that there was any inconsistency in stepping up arms sales while advocating restraint: it was like 'comparing an apple with an orange'. They also emphasised just how useful the war had demonstrated such arms sales to be. Under-Secretary of Defence Paul D Wolfowitz explained: 'We haven't just been loading the Saudis and other Gulf states down, as some have said, with toys they could never use. Those sales made a big difference.'[3]

And there are new apples to sell. The media emphasis on high-tech 'smart' weaponry during the Gulf War masked the continued large-scale use of 'dumb' technology which did not spare civilian lives in Iraq.[4] But the smart weapons played a decisive role. Stealth bombers took Iraqi radar by surprise at the start of the war. Laser-guided bombs pinpointed bridges and bunkers. Tanks and artillery with night-vision outgunned Iraqi equipment with longer range but less accuracy. These successes gave arms manufacturers a much-valued testimonial to rescue production lines threatened by the 'peace dividend' stemming from the reduced rivalry of the Soviet Union. New sales of M-1A1 tanks to the Middle East would save General Dynamics Corporation, the only firm still producing tanks for the US Army, from closing plants in Detroit and Lima, Ohio. Production of McDonnell Douglas's much-publicised tank-killing Apache attack helicopter would also be rescued.[5] As the *New York Times* reported:

> The thrashing that the West's military forces gave President Saddam Hussein of Iraq has whetted the appetite of Third World nations for advanced weapons, military analysts say. One result... could be a rapid advance in accuracy and technological sophistication of the developing world's military arsenals. Having watched as 'smart' bombs and cruise missiles dispatched an armed force that Iraq spent US$50 billion to amass, Third World nations are already scouting for similar weapons... The trend... suggests some erosion in the military edge that enabled Western nations to win so decisively, without heavy casualties to their own forces, in the Gulf War. More important, it raises the prospect that future Third World wars could be vastly more destructive...[6]

Yet the danger of this 'trend' did not at all strengthen the argument for arms control. Measures proposed after the war only concerned 'weapons of mass destruction and the missiles used to deliver them' — chemical, bacteriological and nuclear weapons and their means of delivery. Instead the prospect of Third-World countries acquiring high-tech weapons was used by Secretary of Defence Dick Cheney to justify the need for the US to launch its own new 'military technological revolution'. This, he explained to the House of Representatives' foreign affairs committee on 19 March, 'will help shape the future security environment in ways favourable to us and will help give us capabilities that we are comfortable employing for deterrence or defence against tomorrow's regional aggressors.'

From sanctions to 'overwhelming force'
The speed with which the UN moved to impose economic sanctions on Iraq was first seen as a good omen for peace-keeping operations. But their subsequent marginalisation can only discredit any future resort to the UN Security Council.

The imposition of economic sanctions under Article 41 of the UN Charter was an appropriate response to a clear act of aggression by one member state against another. But the Charter also states that the Security Council, before moving on to institute military sanctions under Article 42, should reach the conclusion that economic sanctions 'would be inadequate or have proved to be inadequate'. No such finding was ever made. And so the UN's first effective exercise in collective security was hijacked by the United States' determination to solve the crisis by war, securing a mandate from the Security Council which left the UN powerless to control or even monitor the way the war was fought. In the words of the former US State Department Middle East specialist Richard Murphy: 'The US was extremely pleased with the smooth functioning of the Security Council up to the war. When the war started in a sense we took over'.[7]

Yet when first imposed, the economic embargo was judged to have had a very good chance of success. 'This is an unprecedented embrace of the sanctions programme', said one senior US official. 'There has never been one that has had the breadth of commitment and coverage as this one'.[8]

Sanctions were regarded as a 'long haul' operation, in the words of Secretary of Defence Dick Cheney. His British counterpart Tom King said that 'it was never going to be a quick fix, a two-week wonder', while even Margaret Thatcher argued that sanctions should be given 'time to work'.[9]

But such statements proved to be a blind, as the troop build-up in Saudi Arabia continued and the high-tech weaponry was prepared. The peaceful route was publicly foreclosed when Mr Bush announced (after the mid-term elections, though the decision had been taken before) the doubling of US troops in the Gulf to half a million. Now forecasts that sanctions might produce a withdrawal by spring or summer 1991 were regarded as proving the need for military force. The troops could not wait that long, and the coalition 'might crumble by then'.[10] The announcement on 8 November was described as an ultimatum to Saddam Hussein: 'Either withdraw from Kuwait within weeks or face US attack.[11]

Almost unobserved, a new military doctrine had been adopted in Washington which would be demonstrated with deadly effect in the war. This was the philosophy of 'invincible' or 'overwhelming' force, which stressed the concentration of enormous quantities of combat power for simultaneous use over a broad front. Mr Bush, said his Defence Secretary, belonged to the 'don't-screw-around school of military strategy'. So did Mr Cheney and his Chief of Staff Colin Powell.

> Two other critical policy-makers in the administration are adherents of the doctrine of overwhelming force: Secretary of State James Baker and National Security Adviser Brent Scowcroft... 'There are five men who believe in their heads and hearts that the remedy is to present maximum firepower,' one senior administration official said last week. The critics can debate the impact of the [economic] sanctions or the diplomacy or the timeliness of the UN resolutions, but that maximisation is the engine driving the train. Period.'[12]

Though Colin Powell stressed the need for 'overwhelming force' on a visit to Britain in early December, this indication of the US attitude to war was missed by the British press, just as it had barely noted the discrepancy between earlier optimism and later pessimism about sanctions. Similarly, evidence that an Iraqi withdrawal might be achieved by face-saving negotiation with Saddam rather than stern ultimatum was relegated to the sidelines of debate.

The rejection of diplomacy

The Gulf War has set a gloomy precedent for negotiation as an alternative to war. And the issue of negotiations with Saddam Hussein was always distorted. The US/British position was that there was nothing to negotiate except Iraq's full and unconditional withdrawal: this was to be the one world crisis where diplomacy had no role. When visitors to Baghdad reported that Saddam would discuss some form of withdrawal, it was denied that he had any such intention.

The truth was that Saddam at first hinted, and later stated more clearly, that the occupation of Kuwait was not irreversible. He wished to exact a price for it, of course, either in the shape of territorial concessions, or in a face-saving 'linkage' to the Palestinian question. But the task of Western diplomacy, backed by sanctions, should have been to whittle down that price to a minimum. Instead, contact with Saddam was discouraged and the British and US embassies were not empowered to discuss these matters in Baghdad. Independent efforts by Western politicians — former West German chancellor Willy Brandt, former British prime minister Edward Heath, and British Labour member of parliament Tony Benn — were derided; and, during the war, the extensive efforts at mediation by President Gorbachev's personal envoy, Yevgeny Primakov, were coolly received. It is not surprising that these initiatives produced only veiled indications of flexibility from Baghdad.

Saddam's propensity for bluff and hard bargaining was already well known and his public offers were masked in rhetoric. Yet the diplomats failed in their professional duty to explore them. His secret proposals were also ignored and the Western media showed a remarkable lack of interest when their contents were revealed.

Two examples, one secret and one public, may be noted here. On 23 August Iraq sent a message to the White House via a former high-ranking US diplomat (probably Richard Murphy). It offered to exchange withdrawal from Kuwait and the release of foreigners for the lifting of sanctions, guaranteed access to the Gulf and sole control of the contested Rumailah oil field. Leading US newspapers failed to cover this story until it was published by the less prestigious *Newsday*. And White House sources, while confirming that the offer had been received, rejected it as incompatible with President Bush's demand for 'unconditional withdrawal'. The offer was then naturally denied in

Baghdad, allowing Western diplomats to query whether it had ever been made.[13]

The second example relates to 17 November when Baghdad published the transcript of an interview with Saddam by the US television network ABC. It was the first public indication that withdrawal from Kuwait was fully negotiable, and that the UN resolution demanding withdrawal need not be contested, provided the issue was linked to the problems of 'the region as a whole' (principally Palestine):

> **Q.** Mr President, when you say that you are ready for dialogue as you said earlier, do you really want dialogue and does this mean that Kuwait is negotiable?
> **A.** When I say something I mean it. I mean every word I say. I said that dialogue must include all the issues in the region based on unified humane, political and legal standards. When it is said, for example, that Iraq must implement the UN Security Council resolutions as they are — resolutions that [it] adopted without a dialogue with Iraq — we say that these resolutions are not the only resolutions issued by the Security Council with regard to the region's issues...
> **Q.** Are you saying that you will be ready to negotiate about withdrawal from Kuwait if the US is prepared to deal decisively with Israel over the occupation of the occupied Arab territories?
> **A.** Yes...[14]

If Iraq were as unremittingly 'intransigent' as claimed, one might have expected Washington to leak the evidence, but the only leak came from Baghdad. Nor did Washington contest the accuracy of Baghdad's transcript of Saddam's meeting before the invasion with US ambassador April Glaspie on 25 July 1990. Ms Glaspie had to wait till after the war before being allowed to claim that the record had been distorted, and that she had not, after all, condoned Iraqi action against Kuwait. Later Baghdad also published a transcript of Saddam's meeting with UN Secretary-General Javier Pérez de Cuéllar on 13 January 1991 just before the allied offensive three days later. It showed Saddam as willing to 'make sacrifices' and discuss withdrawal. At one point he produced a map of Kuwait and asked Mr Pérez de Cuéllar: 'Where should Iraq withdraw to?' The transcript, which threw doubt on the accepted version that the Secretary-General's mission had been a total failure, was also generally ignored.[15]

Whose appeasement?

As the pace of events and the reporting of them speed up in the new technological revolution of the late 20th century, historical memories grow correspondingly shorter. Western governments could not entirely evade disinterment of their shameful record of support for Saddam Hussein in the 1980s, but sought with some success to minimise its significance. Though abundant new evidence on arms-related sales came to light, the subject aroused little editorial interest even in those journals which published the facts. Some evidence was suppressed: a BBC *Panorama* programme on British involvement in Iraq's attempt to acquire 'supergun' technology was 'postponed' indefinitely. Advocates of the war dismissed the revelations on various grounds: 'everyone knows it already' (a common reaction among specialist journalists); 'we cannot go on raking over history' — this on several occasions from historians on British television; and, from government ministers, 'at least we won't make the same mistake again'. Thus could be avoided any serious questioning of the fundamentals of Western foreign policy in the Middle East which had led to the support of more than one dictator and, unless challenged, could do so again.

The record of appeasement went up to the very day of the invasion of Kuwait. It has been argued that US ambassador Glaspie knowingly encouraged Saddam Hussein to invade by assuring him that 'we have no opinion on Arab-Arab conflicts, like your border disagreement with Kuwait. This issue is not associated with America.' This interpretation, however, goes beyond what can be inferred from the transcript. It seems more likely that Ms Glaspie overlooked Saddam's clear signal that intervention might take place because she was trying so hard to adhere to the well-established policy of not offending him. Ms Glaspie was much less culpable than her superior, Assistant Secretary of State John H Kelly, who told Congress a week later, when 100,000 Iraqi troops had already massed on the Kuwaiti border, that economic sanctions against Iraq were unwise and would only be 'costly to American farmers and businessmen'.[16]

In June 1990 Mr Kelly had told Congress that although human rights abuses continued in Iraq, Baghdad was taking 'some modest steps in the right direction'. Violations of human rights, as the post-war fate of the Kurds would show again, were always minimised. After the Halabja gassing of thousands of Kurds in March 1988, Britain extended new trade credits to Iraq. Washington made a token protest but refused to co-sponsor a resolution before the UN Commission on Human Rights.[17] Britain's response to the execution in March 1990 of British journalist Farzad Bazoft was just as shameful. Foreign Secretary Douglas Hurd refused to end trade credits to Iraq, and it was reported that:

> The government has informally relaxed the arms sanctions it imposed during the eight-year Iran-Iraq war in its efforts to ensure that Britain is not left out of the international drive to re-equip the Iraqi regime despite its aggressive reputation. ... 'Everything except

Introduction

things which go bang', as one Whitehall source put it yesterday...Trade was one factor when ministers decided not to step up retaliation for either the execution of the *Observer* journalist Farzad Bazoft or the attempt to smuggle 'nuclear triggers' out of Heathrow.[18]

The only serious critics of Saddam Hussein in the United States and Britain before the invasion of Kuwait were human rights organisations, left-wing bodies and Iraqi exile groups whose protests were ignored. Many of them went on to oppose the allied war, only to be accused of advocating appeasement of Saddam! But the facts show that it was those who went to war who were the real appeasers — and who resumed their old ways as soon as the war ended.

The paradox is clear. The West's conception of 'peace and security' in the Middle East, based upon an undemocratic status quo among its allies and an indefinite tolerance for the denial of Palestinian rights, has not changed. The only alteration during the war was in the cast-list, when Iraq proved a greater liability than asset by striking at the West's economic interests in Kuwait. Nor has the difficulty of establishing the truth in the midst of instant forgetfulness and wilful distortion become much easier since the 'end' of the war. For a whole week in April, Kurdish refugees died on mountainsides along the Turkish border while the international community did nothing to persuade the Turkish government (which was entitled to doubt that it would be given long-term help) to allow them to descend. Very little attention was paid to the much larger numbers who had fled to Iran, or to the fate of the Shi'as in southern Iraq. Though the establishment of an allied 'safe-haven' in northern Iraq would encourage the return of many refugees, this diverted attention from the inadequate efforts being made to put in place a long-term UN relief and peace-keeping operation.

Has the experience of the Gulf War proved so shattering that there will be a salutary rethinking of the Western policies which helped prepare the ground for the conflict? Will the suffering of the Kurds prompt us to cry out loud enough to demand consistent efforts for peace and reconciliation in the area?

The conclusions of the contributors to this volume are generally gloomy. The crisis of the Middle East is certain to continue and likely to get worse. Yet public opinion can be effective if people are able to get past the evasions and lies of governments. This applies as much to the peoples of the region, whose own ruling elites are responsible for so much suffering and so many mistakes, as to ourselves. That is why we seek in this book to offer an alternative and more truthful perspective from which to look beyond the Gulf War.

Notes
1. David Hoffman in *International Herald Tribune*, 15 March 1991
2. Ann Devroy and R Jeffrey Smith, 'Neutrality in Iraq Reaffirmed by US', *Washington Post*, 27 March 1991
3. Don Oberdorfer and R Jeffrey Smith, 'US Faces Contradiction on Mideast Arms Control', *Washington Post*, 7 March 1991
4. Of 88,500 tons of bombs dropped on Iraq and occupied Kuwait, 70 per cent missed their targets, according to Airforce Chief of Staff General Merrill A McPeak. 'Smart' weapons only accounted for 6,520 out of the total tonnage — Barton Gellman in *Washington Post*, 16 March 1991
5. Steven Pearlstein, 'Defence Contractors Lobbying to Keep Weapons Programs Alive', *Washington Post*, 9 March 1991
6. Michael Wines, 'US Arms Dazzle the Third World', *International Herald Tribune*, 27 March 1991
7. *Channel Four News*, London, 25 March 1991
8. Stuart Auerbach, 'Sanctions Rated Cooperative Success; World Commitment on Iraq Embargo Far Exceeds Past US Efforts', *Washington Post*, 1 Sept 1990
9. Associated Press, 15 Oct 1990; *Independent*, 3 Sept 1990
10. R Jeffrey Smith and George Lardner Jr, 'Iraq Sanctions Seen Working Slowly', *Washington Post*, 24 Nov 1990
11. Associated Press 9 Nov 1990
12. Rick Atkinson and Bob Woodward, 'Gulf Turning Points: Strategy, Diplomacy, Prolonged Buildup Reflects Doctrine of Invincible Force', *Washington Post*, 2 Dec 1990
13. Kurt Royce in *Newsday*, 27 Aug 1990; Associated Press, 30 Aug 1990 'Administration Source Claims US Rejection of Secret Iraqi Proposals'; Alexander Cockburn, 'In for the Kill', *New Statesman*, 22 Feb 1991
14. BBC *Summary of World Broadcasts*, ME 2095, 19 Nov 1990
15. *Guardian*, 12 Feb 1991
16. David Hoffman, 'Misjudgment of Saddam Seen; Early Evidence of Bellicosity, Drive for Dominance Noted', *Washington Post*, 8 Aug 1990
17. Middle East Watch, *Human Rights in Iraq*, Yale, 1990, pp113-114
18. Michael White in *Guardian*, 14 April 1990

1
A NEW WORLD ORDER?

How the West mobilised for war

Richard Falk

What lies behind the rhetoric of a New World Order? Was the war a victory for the United Nations, or an abuse of its procedures? Richard Falk, professor of international law at Princeton University, questions popular approval for militarism, and suggests the way forward for peace

It was important after the Cold War to find a new justification for the use of military force overseas, especially in the Third World where US lives might be at risk. The shadow of Vietnam still troubled US policy-makers in the early stages of the Gulf crisis and they feared that the war might end inconclusively. The White House continued to face the problem of mobilising for war in a political democracy. People needed to be convinced that it was worth risking lives, although the task had been made easier by the fact that a professional army could now be relied upon to do the fighting. This was an important factor in the Gulf War. Unlike Vietnam, it was not the conscripted children of the privileged middle classes who would be put at risk. Nevertheless, to build political support for the war, an ideological justification other than anti-communism was necessary.

President Reagan had tried to build such an ideological foundation through figures like Colonel Quadaffi and other anti-US leaders, classifying their governments as supporters of 'terrorism'. But while this line of argument enjoyed some success, and was enough to justify a surprise military attack on Libya in 1986, it could not provide an ideological substitute for the Cold War. Indeed, several forces in US society had blocked the apparent intention of the Reagan administration to intervene directly in Nicaragua. Despite the popularity of the Reagan presidency, there was strong resistance to intervention from the public, from within the armed forces (especially the army) and from the Catholic Church. Such opposition from the army and Church marked a significant change from the Vietnam era. The

Church, for example, had then been united behind US policy (in fact, President Ngo Dinh Diem of South Vietnam was a devout Catholic who had been groomed for leadership by Cardinal Spellman while in exile in the United States). And when it came to the 1990 Gulf crisis, the US army was worried at the possibility of an unsuccessful military intervention in the Middle East and being saddled with the blame, in the manner of Vietnam, for the failures of the politicians and the civilian population. It was therefore necessary to find a new justification for war and win it quickly with the minimum loss of life.

Manipulation of the UN

In this sense the United Nations played a major role in the build-up to the war, but not subsequently. The claim that this was a UN war worked well with both the European and US public, reinforced by the presentation of Saddam Hussein as a leader who personified evil and had built up a dangerous war machine. It was seen as a good war, perhaps the first good war since the Second World War, and certainly since the Korean War 40 years earlier. It had received UN blessing and the organisation's formal procedures had been followed. When Mr Bush first put forward the idea of the New World Order, many believed, somewhat naively, that such rhetoric expressed a genuine desire for the UN to be used in the way originally as intended following its establishment in 1945; namely, as an instrument of collective security in response to an act of aggression. Such a collective response was understood as an alternative both to appeasement, which had failed to stop Hitler in the pre-Second World War period, and to a deliberate policy of war.

From this perspective such a middle path included three elements in the case of Kuwait: defensive military capabilities (to contain Iraq after 2 August), economic sanctions (to force withdrawal) and diplomatic negotiations (to persuade Iraq to withdraw and facilitate the process). It seemed to many to be an effective and constructive way of restoring Kuwait's sovereignty, and did not rule out military action if the Security Council found, in accordance with Article 41, that sanctions had failed. Kuwait was the first country since the UN's foundation to have been so violently annexed with the intention of destroying it as a distinct state. The situation had to be reversed both for the sake of Kuwait and to restore confidence in UN machinery for collective security. It was important to capitalise on the political consensus that had recently emerged among the body's leading member states.

But as the 15 January deadline approached, it became increasingly clear that a quite different politics lay behind the use of the UN and the rhetoric of a New World Order: that the main US concern was not to get Iraq out of Kuwait but to demonstrate in the post-Cold War world that the United States was able and willing to guarantee the interests of 'world capitalism' and uphold the security concerns of the industrialised world. Geopolitically the Gulf War can be seen as the first resource war of the new international era. It also finessed the perceived 'danger' that the end of the Cold War would produce a so-called 'peace dividend' that would weaken the Pentagon and the military in American society, and lead to a shift in international relations from security to economics — that is, the area where the United States is weak in relation to Japan and Europe. It is not surprising that in early January the White House let it be known that the prospect of Iraq withdrawing from Kuwait before the deadline was a 'nightmare scenario'.

The UN was not used to achieve a peaceful diplomatic solution but to overcome political and moral resistance to a policy of war. There is a lot to be said about the UN's failure to maintain its independence and its evident willingness to allow itself to be shamelessly manipulated as a vehicle of US foreign policy and geopolitical ambition. It was deeply disappointing that the Secretary-General did not object to the abuse of Security Council procedures and even allowed himself to be used in a manner that cut directly against the grain of the UN Charter and its concern with the avoidance of war. It would have been an extremely important message to the world, particularly the Third World, if Mr Pérez de Cuéllar had resigned in January or the following weeks when it became clear that he was not being allowed to act appropriately as the chief officer of the UN, and that the Security Council was not carrying out its proper supervisory role.

The UN was denied a major opportunity to use its procedures to uphold its fundamental mandate to save successive generations from the scourge of war. Under extreme and different circumstances, of course, the Security Council might have authorised military measures against Iraq to restore Kuwaiti sovereignty in accordance with the UN Charter, setting out clear goals and restrictions. But it should be noted that the sanctions against Iraq already had a military element since authorisation had been given for their enforcement by means of a blockade. A blockade is considered an act of war under international law.

In the actual use of force, as permitted by Security Council Resolution 678, two of the Charter's basic requirements were completely evaded. Firstly, according to Article 42, military measures can only be taken if the Security Council has found that other measures have failed. In other words, before the vote on Resolution 678 on 29 November a formal decision should have been made that sanctions and diplomacy had been tried for a sufficient period of time and had not worked. Secondly, the article states that military measures, once authorised by the Security Council, should be specific and that the UN has a basic responsibility to supervise them. And in this instance, the measures should have been tied to the concrete steps needed to get Iraqi forces out of Kuwait with the minimum loss of life on all sides and the minimum damage to the civilian population.

While there might have been disagreement as to how these objectives could have been achieved, their relevance should have been beyond dispute. Indeed, it was clearly illegitimate for the Security Council to give the United States and its loosely-based coalition what became an unrestricted mandate to wage war, with absolute discretion to determine the goals and level of violence as the conflict progressed. The UN Secretary-General had ample grounds on which to oppose the drift to war in December and January. Such a display of independence would have sent a powerful, if inflammatory, warning to Washington and elsewhere that the chief officer of the UN had a totally different interpretation of collective security and the UN Charter from that expressed by Resolution 678 or the war itself.[1]

But once it had given the mandate, the UN was predictably marginalised, as was most of the coalition. Even Kuwait was reduced to a minor player during the course of the war. Decisions over what to do, how to fight, what weapons to use, how far to carry the mandate, were all made by the White House, a few advisors and the main military commanders. This usurpation of authority was not challenged by the other members of the coalition except indirectly and in the most discreet manner. The Soviet Union did seek to avoid a ground war with its February peace initiative; and, in response, the Iraqi government, including Saddam Hussein, did show a clear willingness to withdraw promptly and unconditionally from Kuwait — alleged, even by Bush, to be the sole purpose of the war. But the White House had its own plans and did not at all welcome the Soviet effort. It made no attempt to hide its concern that unilateral withdrawal by Iraq would undermine its real aims.[2] And the real aim of the war, the definition of which had been influenced by Israel from the outset, was to destroy Iraq's status in the region as a strong military and political force.

Deception of public opinion

One can argue from a geopolitical point of view that Saddam Hussein was an evil, aggressive leader, that his war machine was dangerous to the region, and that it was likely to become more so in the years ahead. But it should be understood that this argument was not made either in the Security Council, to the American people, or to win support from the other governments that participated in the war. It poses a very serious problem for political democracy when leaders deliberately deceive the public about the true nature of what they are proposing to achieve by military force. And the problem becomes even more serious when the public endorses the deception by welcoming so enthusiastically the victorious result. It encourages future leaders to use whatever manipulative means they can to build support for their aims and avoid debate.

In early January it was proving very difficult in the United States to build such a consensus around the abandonment of sanctions and the need for war — until the issue was taken out of its Kuwaiti setting. In December Bush raised, for the first time, the threat that Iraq was about to become a nuclear power as a reason for war. The argument quickly shifted public opinion. Bush started off by claiming that Iraq was likely to obtain nuclear weapons in a decade. Then the interval was reduced to five years, then to one year — and then, Iraq might even have a few crude bombs already! It was the fastest example of weapons acquisition in human history, demonstrating an unprecedented technological capability in Baghdad. Such claims were a public-relations manipulation. No documentation was ever provided to back them up and concern about incipient nuclearism disappeared almost entirely from public discourse after the war had started.

What is so disturbing about this whole pattern is that very few influential voices were to be heard anywhere objecting to the manipulation of both the UN and of world public opinion. The war has succeeded politically in the United States beyond the wildest dreams of its planners. No US president can receive the 91 per cent approval-rate that Bush temporarily enjoyed — not even Jesus.

Such enthusiasm for victory in war poses fundamental questions for the future. For the political culture of constitutional democracies in the industrialised world would appear to be comfortable with the North's use of violence in the South of the world. The initial reluctance to go to war with Iraq was not a reluctance to kill others or to project US military power, but a fear that war would not work, would be divisive and expensive, and would lead to a loss of American lives. The Vietnam syndrome that Bush complained about was not an objection to military intervention in the Third World, but to unsuccessful military intervention. The Iraqi military machine had been presented as the fourth largest in the world. So when the US-led allies scored such a comprehensive and spectacular military victory with what were referred to as 'miraculously low casualties', the Rambo mentality achieved full expression in the United States and Britain. The war became a demonstration of the vitality and technological superiority of the two societies. This was especially important in the United States, as it countered the country's growing sense of inferiority in relation to Japan and to Europe.

Dividends of war

The editorials of the *Wall Street Journal* — perhaps the best barometer of the thinking of the US economic and political establishment these days — were clear from the start. The first editorial in support of the war was called 'A Declining Power'. It stated that it was important that aggression should not work and that the sovereignty of Kuwait should be re-established, adding that it was even more important that the West should ensure access to oil at tolerable prices. But the crucial thing, the editorial went on, was that the United States should decide that it had a mission and identity in the world. This war was not about Kuwait or about the world, but about America.[3] The editorial after the temporary ceasefire was called 'This Remarkable Victory'[4] which saw the victory on the desert battlefields as a ringing vindication of US technological prowess and managerial technique. Japan might make better consumer goods but what counted most in the world was who made the best weapons. Weapons and their proper use were the makers of history and the United States had given a decisive demonstration to Europe and the Soviet Union that the weapons it produced were by far the most effective and powerful.

The popularity of the Gulf War has confirmed one's worst fears about the political culture that has emerged in the West, carrying to its logical extreme the whole pattern of global conflict since 1945. For it is in the South where all the significant fighting and dying has occurred. The only exceptions, and they are minor by comparison, have been the conflict in Northern Ireland, the Soviet intervention in Hungary in 1956 which cost a thousand lives, and the Turkish intervention in Cyprus in 1974 which took several thousand lives.

It is mainly sophisticated diplomatic historians who regard the period since the Second World War as 'the long peace'. John Lewis Gaddis, one of the most careful analysts of the strategy behind the Cold War, has argued that it had given Europe and the North the longest period of peace since ancient times.[5] The long peace was quite compatible with the idea that geopolitical wars between East and West to ensure the dominance of the North could be fought indefinitely in the Third World.

Indeed, many wars took place. But the level of casualties suggested anything but long peace — some 30 million deaths in Asia, Africa and Latin America. The wars were all fought with weapons produced in the North and often with intervention on one or both sides by competing northern states. The South was also used as a battlefield to test new weapons allowing the North to displace its conflicts or keep them within safe limits — safe for the North that is. John Mueller has argued in an important book published shortly before the Gulf War, *Retreat from Doomsday:The Obsolescence of Major War*,[6] that the experience in the period between the First World War to the Cold War convinced the leaders of the North that war was too costly — but not too costly in and against the South.

17

This is why the Vietnam syndrome was so important before the Gulf War. Vietnam, Afghanistan, and to some extent Korea, had led to growing concern that the use of military force in the South had failed in its political objectives and that war itself had become a flawed instrument of statecraft. Victory in the Gulf would appear to contradict this experience and to have re-established that a political consensus can be built in a democratic society around intervention, provided it is successful. It has also reinforced the idea that the latest high-tech weapons can win decisively and with a low loss of life, even against well-armed opponents. And most amazing of all, the United States has found a way of waging a major war and getting others to pay for it.[7] Not only has the United States become a well-paid mercenary and guardian, but it can also look ahead to the largest share of the contracts to rebuild the countries that have been destroyed. It is the first war in history where the countries taking part openly and unashamedly competed for a share of the reconstruction contracts and the size of their share would appear to have been determined by the degree to which they contributed to the destruction: the more the destruction, the more the profits. One journalist explains how Italy, because it had not destroyed very much in Kuwait, would not get much construction work, in spite of having some of the best qualified companies.[8]

During the war the coalition leaders, including the White House, claimed to have learned the danger of selling high-tech weapons to the Third World, as well as the need for a stringent regime of arms control, especially in the Middle East. But the fighting had barely stopped when President Bush and Secretary of State Baker said that it would be unrealistic to restrict most arms sales to the region. It was also implied that an unprecedented opportunity now existed to increase the market share of US weapons, given their impressive performance in the war. Such expansion was becoming increasingly important as budget constraints made US arms producers more dependent than previously on exports.[9] While no one in the Third World now wants to buy Soviet weapons or even French weapons, substantial orders are now arriving for cruise missiles and Patriot missiles. And the companies making them are a good investment. So instead of the 'peace dividend' that was expected in 1989, there is a 'war dividend' with the prospect of increasing arms sales, including to the Middle East. Iraq may even become a valued customer again, though that will take a little time.

Alliances of convenience

Yet geopolitics is rarely stable, especially in the Middle East. Since the ceasefire there have been signs of a debate in Washington as to whether it would be better to keep Saddam Hussein in power, given the uncertainty of alternatives produced by the internal conflict in Iraq which could lead either to the disintegration of the country or to an extension of Iranian influence. Saddam, who was so recently compared to Hitler, is again the preferred political option, at least for the moment. Indeed, the coalition forces made a clear, deliberate choice to allow his Republican Guard back into Iraq to confront the Shi'a rebels in Basra. The rebels were now seen as the main threat because a victory by them would benefit Iran regionally. Before the bodies of Iraqi war victims had even been buried, the United States was manipulating in the cruellest and most cynical way the political destiny of a country it had just destroyed — supposedly to deal with the evil threat of Saddam Hussein. And such a diplomatic turnabout is likely to be repeated several more times in the end-game phase of the Gulf War, as competing US interests are threatened.

It is the latest chapter of a depressing history. For decades the United States supported Islamic fundamentalism as the best way to counter left-wing influence in the region, particularly in Iran where the CIA financed fundamentalists to neutralise Marxists who were regarded as the main threat to the Shah's rule. But when the Khomeini Islamic revolution succeeded, fundamentalism became overnight the greatest danger and Washington encouraged Iraq, despite its Soviet orientation and the socialist pretensions of the Ba'ath Party, to go to war against Iran in 1980. The United States provided intelligence to Baghdad claiming that the latter could gain a quick victory. Nominally neutral, the United States stood to one side in the face of Iraqi aggression and in effect backed Saddam in the 1980-88 Iraq-Iran war. The Gulf War arose mainly because Iraq had come to be seen as a growing threat to Western interests in the region. But who will the next enemy be, and who will be built up to destroy the latest threat? While such a process may not be strange to students of geopolitics, it is a horror story for the peoples of the Middle East, especially the poor.

So far the New World Order has meant a reassertion of the North's military dominance under US leadership, a cynical disregard of the UN, and a confident sense that what was done in the desert could tomorrow be repeated in the jungle — that the high-tech weapons that worked so well against Iraq in the open could be extended to any terrain or opponent in the Third World. And night vision and precision-guided missiles can be adapted for jungle and mountain use. President Bush said during the war that he had recovered his confidence in Star Wars technology but that the latter should not have an East-West purpose. It was Utopian to believe that Star Wars could be used as a shield against a major nuclear adversary, but it made sense in a North-South context. With the militarisation of space under US control, the South could never inflict damage on the North. The North would have total control through surveillance and be able to launch an attack anywhere in the world in a matter of minutes. The North does not want the South to be weak militarily; it wants sufficient regional rivalry in the South with key players to buy the weaponry and provide a continuous market. For the weakest economies in the North are those which most depend on arms exports. And the main arms sellers are not Japan and Germany but the United States, France, Britain and, for that matter, the Soviet Union, China and North Korea.

In the aftermath of the Gulf War, the US government and its closest allies have expressed an idealistic intention to bring peace and security to this tormented region. So far these claims have been no more than that and their credibility will be tested by several issues.

Towards an agenda for peace

Firstly, the issue of self-determination. A more fluid situation has been created and now is the logical moment for pressure on Israel to meet its obligations under international law over the Palestinian issue and the continued occupation of the West Bank and Gaza.

This means an end to the establishment of settlements and land occupations, an end to the collective punishment of whole communities and to the deportation of politically active Palestinians. But it also means implementation of the land-for-peace formula under UN Security Council Resolutions 242 and 338 on Israeli withdrawal and Resolution 181 on the establishment of a Palestinian homeland. A Camp David-style agreement with vague promises and empty rhetoric must not be allowed to substitute for a proper settlement for the Palestinians. The question of Kurdish rights, both in Iraq and elsewhere, must also be seriously addressed; and Lebanon's political sovereignty must be restored in relation to Syria and Israel. Further afield, but still part of a genuine peace process in the area, would be the restoration of the territorial integrity of Cyprus, which would require the withdrawal of Turkish troops.

The second element in any peace process in the Middle East would involve measures to prevent the revival of a regional arms race fuelled by unrestricted arms sales. Initially, this would mean encouraging a regime prohibiting weapons of mass destruction in the region. But such a regime would have to include Israel to be effective and long-term demilitarisation requires a comprehensive settlement of the Arab-Israeli dispute, guaranteed by outside states, especially by the United States and the main European powers. The United States and Europe could give a clear sign of commitment to such a regional process by withdrawing their forces from the Gulf and discarding current plans to establish permanent US bases there.

The third issue relates to post-war reconstruction. This should deal with the environmental catastrophe caused by the burning of more than 500 oil wells set on fire in Kuwait which is likely to affect many countries.

Reconstruction should also restore essential services in Iraq and avoid a punitive 'peace' that would make the Iraqi people pay for years for the dreadful criminality of an unelected tyrant.

The fourth element would involve providing relief for the countries indirectly affected by the Gulf War, either through damage from polluted air and water or through reduced foreign-exchange earnings because of lost remittances from nationals working abroad.

The fifth element involves the future of the UN. In spite of current White House thinking, the opportunity exists for some sort of collective security mechanism to be institutionalised. This would involve the establishment of clear guidelines for the application of 'military measures' under Article 42 of the UN Charter, and the revival of long dormant plans for a Military Staff Committee which would co-ordinate and monitor UN peacekeeping efforts (under Articles 46 and 47), as well as to earmark some standby forces in advance.

At present, the outlook is bleak in all five areas. The 'peace' process, like the war itself, is aimed at safeguarding Western interests in the Middle East by economic, political, and military means. And, above all, that means protecting oil supplies and maintaining the status quo vis-à-vis Israel.

It is crucial for those in Europe and North America who opposed the war to continue their struggle to publicise the real issues that lay behind it. For the war and its aftermath are of fundamental significance to the peoples of the Middle East, to North-South relations, and to Christian-Muslim dialogue. The peace movement faces an unprecedented challenge in its efforts to put forward positive, persuasive proposals for achievement of global security and world justice.

We should also have no illusions about the degree to which the people will oppose state militarism in a democratic society. Victory in the Gulf War met with such popular enthusiasm that the phenomenon cannot be explained away simply as the inevitable effect of state propaganda or media manipulation. The political culture of the industrialised North embraces successful wars of domination and exploitation, particularly those with a racial or religious overtone, and this has disturbing implications for the free functioning of constitutional democracy. Believers in the North in the potential of democracy must not only support the struggle of peoples in the Middle East for human and democratic rights. We must also seek to remedy the deformations that have crept into our own political culture, reinforcing militarism and a supremacist worldview.

Notes
1. There are indications that Mr Pérez de Cuéllar actually entertained some of these feelings, and even expressed them to a certain extent during his meeting with

Saddam Hussein in Baghdad days before the deadline expired. See text of partial transcript as released by Iraq, *The Guardian*, 12 Feb 1991, p2; also John J Goldman, 'From Iraq, a Hussein-Pérez de Cuéllar Transcript', *International Herald Tribune*, 13 Feb 1991, p1

2. According to one report, Mr Bush was 'biting his lip' to contain his anger over Gorbachev's unwelcome diplomatic efforts, and that the Soviet president had, in the words of a White House insider, done 'more harm to himself' in Washington by the peace initiative 'than he did by all the head-knocking in the Baltics.' Jack Nelson, 'Gorbachev Plan Risks Ties With US, Analysts Say,' *International Herald Tribune*, 22 Feb 1991, p3

3. The phrase 'a declining power' was a sarcastic reference to the contention of Paul Kennedy in his book *The Rise and Fall of the Great Powers* that the United States had entered a period of 'relative decline'. The point of the editorial, and subsequent discussion, was to insist that the American success in the Gulf War was a decisive refutation to the decline thesis. 'A Declining Power,' *Wall Street Journal Europe*, 18-19 Jan 1991, p8

4. For the celebratory text see 'This Remarkable Victory,' *Wall Street Journal Europe*, 4 March 1991, p10

5. Gaddis, 'The Long Peace: Elements of Stability in the Postwar International System', *International Security*, Vol 10, No 4 (Spring 1986), pp 99-142

6. Mueller, *Retreat from Doomsday: The Obsolescence of Major War*, New York, Basic Books, 1989

7. According to *Fortune* figures the cost of the war to the United States has been US$47.5 billion and the value of the pledges comes to US$53.5 billion (mainly from Kuwait, Saudi Arabia, Germany, Japan).*Fortune*, 25 March 1991, p28. Some assessments are even more favourable to the United States. Congressional budget appraisals place the cost of the war at only US$40 billion. 'With Quick Victory, US Is Staring at a Profit on War', *International Herald Tribune*, 27 March 1991

8. Michael C Bergmeijer, 'Italy Lags in Race for Contracts From Kuwaitis', *Wall Street Journal Europe*, 4 March 1991, p6

9. Perhaps this point is obscure. If domestic demands for expensive weaponry declines, the economics of profitable arms production may require additional sales elsewhere. To maintain 'a product line', a certain number of units must be sold to

From the cauldron of war to the chaos of peace

Alain Gresh

The Middle East region faces not tranquillity but a period of prolonged upheaval, argues Alain Gresh. To stop the cycle of hatred would require a transformation of US policy. But although Mr Bush may want a Palestinian settlement, who will put pressure on Israel to achieve it?

With their systematic bombing of Iraq and their determination to eliminate Saddam Hussein's power at all cost, the United States broke all constraints imposed by United Nations resolutions. Now, after the heat of battle, a post-war order is being created which threatens to be even more unstable and unjust. According to the White House, the only obstacle to an otherwise glorious tomorrow in the Middle East was Iraq, to be dealt with by 'the total destruction of Iraq's military infrastructure, weapons development factories, missile sites, and as many tanks, airplanes and artillery pieces as possible. The goal was to render Iraq unable to project power beyond its borders for years to come... irrespective of whether it gets out of Kuwait'.[1] And what did it matter if this goal ignored the constraints of UN resolutions, when it would supposedly hasten the emergence of a 'new order' based on peace and co-existence?

There are many observers who do not share this idyllic post-war vision. One of them has asked whether the coalition can ignore 'the seething nationalist and religious passions bubbling below. These could boil up in America's face and scar it for a hundred years'.[2] Now that America's formidable war machine has crushed its adversary, what are the likely consequences for Iraq and the region as a whole? The disintegration of the regime in power in Baghdad since 1968 and monopolised by Saddam Hussein, who has systematically silenced all dissent, would create a worrying vacuum in the country. The main institutions would fall apart, including the army, which, once defeated, would lose its legitimacy. And the exiled opposition, from the communists to the Muslim fundamentalists, although united by circumstances, has lost contact with a population depoliticised by the dictatorship. Anarchy and disorder would threaten to take over. Romania would seem a haven of peace by comparison. Any new authorities would have to deal with destructive, centrifugal tendencies, which would dispute the monopoly of power wielded since the creation of the Iraqi state by the Sunni minority. In other words, the Shi'a majority, which was for a time susceptible to the appeal of Khomeinism, or the three million Kurds who have repeatedly raised the banner of revolt against the central authorities. Will the Iraqi state — an artificial creation, like all those born from the dismemberment of the Middle East — survive these cracks?

A state of anarchy in Iraq would rekindle the ambitions of its powerful neighbouring states. Turkey, for example — which has aligned itself with the United States and which, according to Prime Minister Ozal, hopes to 'come out of the crisis a strong power' — is facing its own Kurdish insurrection. Ankara could, as in the Iran-Iraq war, invoke its right to pursue *peshmergas* (Kurdish fighters) into Iraq, or even resurrect its claims to the province of Mosul, ceded to Iraq in 1925 by the League of Nations (the UN's precursor). In Iran, the struggles within the leadership intensified during the war; the radical faction denounced the government's 'murderous silence' in face of 'the military expedition launched by world blasphemy, with the United States at its head'. But after the war ended, Tehran intervened on the side of the Iraqi Shi'as.

Regional instabilities
Saudi Arabia, pillar of the anti-Saddam Hussein camp, will not be spared by what threatens to be a prolonged upheaval. The Wahhabi dynasty has shown itself to be unable to protect its own security — a fact which will not be changed by its decision to increase the size of its army from 65,000 to 90,000 men, or buy US$7 billion worth of arms from the United States. With one quarter of the planet's oil reserves, the world's major oil exporter will now depend on the US military presence or on surrogate Egyptian and Syrian forces. Such a situation led to the expression of considerable anxiety during the war and provoked fierce internal opposition, fuelled by the exorbitant cost that maintaining these foreign forces would require. Underground religious groups stepped up their attacks and cassettes were circulated clandestinely. According to one preacher, 'The hostility between Islam and the West is a lasting reality. That is why it is a mistake to appeal to the Westerners to defend us.'[3] The unity of the various provinces remains fragile. The eastern province of al-Hasa, where the oil wells are concentrated, has historical links with Iraq and Bahrain, and even with Iran and India; it has a large oppressed

Shi'a community which has erupted in violent demonstrations against the regime on several recent occasions, most notably in 1978-79.

On the eve of his death in 1953, King Ibn Saud, the founder of the kingdom, is said to have gathered his sons together and told them: 'For us, all the good things and all the bad will come from Yemen.' Whether true or not, this story confirms the Al Saud family's sensitivity to the slightest agitation in its southern neighbour. The unification of North and South Yemen in May 1990 — an event of major importance which drastically upset the balance of power in the peninsula — had already given rise to noticeable disquiet in Riyadh: the new state has a population twice the size of Saudi Arabia. To punish the Sanaa government for its hostility to the US presence, Saudi Arabia expelled over 500,000 Yemeni workers, thus aggravating a historical dispute marked by serious border disagreements. Can the Saudi regime meet these challenges and that presented by the Sanaa regime as it introduces reforms such as a multiparty system and freedom of the press?

The irony is that it is those states which expressed reservations about the Gulf War that have recently adopted relatively solid measures in favour of democracy: Yemen, Algeria, Tunisia and Jordan.

The crisis has plunged Jordan into a fierce economic recession.[4] The mobilisation of the population (over half of which is of Palestinian origin) behind Saddam Hussein during the war intensified, as radical Palestinian or fundamentalist groups became an established presence and demanded arms to do battle with the 'Zionist enemy'. On 1 January 1991 the Muslim Brotherhood entered the government. This tide of feeling (so far checked by the multiparty system and nascent democracy) and the tensions between Jordanians and Palestinians (who remain second-class citizens) could lead to the implosion of a monarchy traditionally close to the West or lead to a coup d'etat. And, for their part, Israeli members of parliament have already demanded the creation of a security zone east of the Jordan river, similar to that under the control of the Israeli army in south Lebanon.[5]

What will become of the Palestine Liberation Organisation, weakened by the assassination of two of its top leaders, Abu Iyad and Abu al-Hol, in Tunis on 14 January 1991, and by its decision to support Saddam Hussein? The Israeli government has so far failed in its long-standing attempts to destroy the PLO. And during the three-year *intifada* (uprising) in the occupied territories, the PLO has managed to channel the anger of Palestinian youth at the continued denial of the Palestinians' basic rights now further inflamed by the massive influx of Soviet Jews. But when Arafat and his colleagues come to be replaced, it seems very unlikely that 'moderate' notables, ready to negotiate with the Jewish state, will again emerge from a population that has reached breaking point. Indeed, terrorist groups like that of Abu Nidal or radical Muslim

25

fundamentalists are much more likely candidates to take over from the PLO.

From Syria to Egypt, from the Gulf to North Africa, the systematic destruction of a brother country has provoked anger and indignation, whatever their feelings towards Saddam Hussein. Not since the end of the Second World War and the creation of the state of Israel in 1948 have there been such deep divisions within the Arab world. And the wave of popular opposition may grow — a mixture of reinvigorated Arab nationalism and anti-establishment Islam, feeding off economic and social inequalities, the persistence of archaic, anti-democratic systems (supported by the West), the monopoly control of oil wealth by comic-opera emirates, and the squandering of resources on useless high-tech weapons and investments abroad. Every bomb that fell on Iraq, every Scud missile launched against Israel or Saudi Arabia, deepened the gulf between the two shores of the Mediterranean, between the Arab-Islamic and Western civilisations. And the danger exists that this gulf will widen after the war, unless the West moves to resolve the problems of the Middle East, beginning with the Palestinian issue.

American goals

US officials were strangely silent on such dangers when the war was in progress and this point was stressed by the US press: the White House had been too busy preparing for war and had 'done relatively little thinking about the shape of peace in the Gulf'.[6] Such negligence leaves one agape at the political vision of the country claiming world leadership. US Secretary of State James Baker made only one concrete proposal, put forward in September 1990. He hoped to establish 'new security structures for the region... This would entail maintaining some military presence there.' Christened Gulfo by US journalist Flora Lewis (after Nato), this alliance seemed designed to preserve the status quo rather than attack the roots of the current imbalances. Its first initiative was the agreement signed in March 1991 between the Gulf Co-operation Council, Egypt and Syria.

Moreover, the old American dream of enroling the Middle Eastern states in a military pact has always come up against the insoluble Arab-Israeli conflict. This is a major obstacle and will remain so as long as Washington refuses to implement international law and apply the UN resolutions that the United States itself voted for: General Assembly Resolution 181 (1947) on the partition of Palestine and the creation of two states, one Jewish and the other Arab; and Resolution 191 (1949) on the right of Palestinian refugees to return to their homes and to financial compensation.

In every crisis the United States has been on Israel's side and against the Arab states — in June 1967, just as in October 1973. Even during the Israeli invasion of Lebanon in June 1982, Washington was lenient towards the Jewish state. Washington's identification with the aims of successive Israeli governments, and its obstinate rejection of an international conference on the Arab-Israeli conflict, explains the anti-Americanism of the Arab peoples, who have long been convinced that the ideals proclaimed by the White House over the Middle East smack of oil.

In September 1950, when the Middle East's oil reserves already equalled those of the rest of the world (and were double those of the United States), a US State Department memorandum stressed that 'control of this source of energy, important in peace and war, is a desirable goal in itself... The US Government should seek maximum development in US-owned concessions'.[7]

This craving for black gold had already led Washington to destabilise Mossadegh's regime in Iran because he had dared to commit the *lese-compagnie* of nationalising the oil companies. In return for the CIA'S good offices, US firms obtained 40 per cent of the shares in the Anglo-Iranian Oil Company.[8] According to Washington, all necessary means were to be used to protect low-cost supplies — except negotiations with the producers. At the time of the first oil shock in 1973, the Ford administration had already considered plans to take control of the Middle East's oil wells. On 14 January 1975 Defence Secretary James Schlesinger declared that 'military operations might be conducted if the need arose'. A more measured editorial in the *New York Times* of 10 January 1975 noted, with foresight, that such a military operation would be 'militarily feasible but politically disastrous'. And the plans were wisely kept under wraps. It is true that the Vietnam war was not yet over...

After the fall of the Shah of Iran in 1979, President Jimmy Carter declared that the Gulf was 'a region of vital interest for the survival of Western Europe, the Far East and finally the United States'. He speeded up the creation of a rapid deployment force, transformed by President Reagan into the US Central Command, whose strength soon reached half a million men. It was first to be deployed in 1987 against Iran and alongside none other but Iraq! One obstacle remained, as John C Ausland, a former State Department employee, has pointed out: 'Most countries in the region were content to benefit from the American umbrella, but no one was willing to host Central Command. So it was installed on McDill Airbase in Florida with a small advance point in the Gulf fleet.'[9] Saudi Arabia, in particular, refused to have any foreign military presence on its territory. The present crisis has provided a long-sought pretext to abandon these reservations.

What will the US make of military victory? To stop the cycle of hatred would require a major shift in US policy, beginning with the convening of an international conference on the region. Strong pressure would also be needed to force the Israeli government to comply with UN Security Council resolutions and to recognise the national rights of the Palestinians.

Some commentators believe that the alliance between Washington and the moderate Arab regimes, forged in blood, will favour such a development. It is an old idea first devised in 1973 by the then President of Egypt Anwar Sadat. But it has never taken concrete shape. Indeed, Israeli Prime Minister Yitzhak Shamir, basking in the glow of praise for his 'moderation' over the Iraqi Scud attacks, has, according to one of his advisers, expressed his belief that 'not only will Israel not have to pay the price in a post-war settlement (which means that it will not leave the occupied territories) but will come out with the upper hand' in the crisis.[10] An enfeebled Soviet Union, a crushed Iraq, a destabilised Jordan and a weakened PLO have all increased the imbalance of power; this can only strengthen the intransigence of the Jewish state. Yet despite this chaotic picture, US policy-makers have spoken optimistically of a more stable and peaceful Middle East.

A new Middle East initiative?

On 6 March President Bush said the United States would now move to solve the problems of the Middle East especially the Arab-Israeli dispute. His speech did contain positive aspects and many long-standing supporters of the Palestinian cause believe that the war was both necessary and a first step towards a more just Middle East. But what is meant by a more just Middle East? Firstly, stable countries, but also a solution to the Arab-Israeli and Lebanese conflicts, and greater democracy and social justice. The United States argued that Iraq's power under Saddam was a threat to the stability of the whole region. But it went on not just to defeat Saddam but to destroy the country itself; it has not just virtually annihilated the Iraqi army but destabilised the country for the next 15 or 20 years. There is also the danger of intervention from neighbouring countries. The West helped Iraq for eight years in the 1980-88 war in the Gulf helping Saddam to wreak destruction on Iran and making it easier for him to then shift his attention to Kuwait. But now the West has destroyed Iraq, who will act as a counterbalance to Iranian and Turkish ambitions? And it is not inconceivable that within a few years the West could be helping another Iraqi leader against external destabilisation.

Jordan also faces a highly dangerous situation after the war. King Hussein is not seen as strongly anti-Western in the Middle East, but throughout the crisis the United States and Saudi Arabia openly sought to destabilise Jordan including through an economic blockade, leading to extreme tension in the country which has favoured the most radical tendencies. The Palestinians may see no alternative but to side with these forces, and such a path could lead to war by Israel with Jordan, as has been openly forecast by voices within the Israeli establishment. They argue not only that Jordan is a Palestinian state but that it is better to have Palestinians in power than King Hussein. During the crisis some right-wing Israeli deputies called for an Israeli security zone inside Jordan as in southern Lebanon.

Mr Bush may be sincere in his current desire for a solution to the Palestinian-Israeli crisis, as a Palestinian state on the West Bank and Gaza no longer poses a major problem for Washington. The United States now enjoys total hegemony in the region and a solution to the Palestinian problem could be helpful. But how can such a solution be achieved? And what was the result of three years of talks with the United States, following the PLO's 1988 decision to recognise Israel? For years the PLO had been told by Western governments to accept the various UN resolutions. But when it finally did, the Americans were unable even to implement their own 'Baker plan' for a limited solution. It should be remembered that Saddam Hussein's popularity among Arab people stemmed from the failure to resolve the Palestinian issue. The Israeli writer Amos Kenan, commenting on a string of European delegations to thank the Shamir government for its 'restraint' during the Gulf War, asked why they were coming to Israel. If there had been negotiations at the beginning of 1990 in Cairo between Israel and a Palestinian delegation accepted by the PLO, he argued, the war would never have happened. It was Shamir's rejection of any solution, which had made it possible for Saddam Hussein to claim that he alone could change the balance of forces in the region allowing a solution of the Palestinian problem.

Can any change in the US administration's policy towards Israel now be detected? Will it apply real pressure against the Israeli government? French Defence Minister Pierre Joxe has said that the problem could be solved if there were the same determination to see to the enforcement of Palestinian rights as there was to liberate Kuwait. And the problem could be solved with just ten per cent of the same determination! But what concrete steps has the United States taken? Four days before the war ended it voted for US$400 million for the construction of homes for Jewish immigrants without demanding any guarantee that the immigrants would not go to East Jerusalem or to the West Bank. Ten days after the war US$670 million were approved to compensate Israel for war damages. And no one refused to talk with the Israeli government because of the inclusion of an extremist minister in the cabinet who advocates the expulsion of all Palestinians. Yet the US refused to talk with the PLO executive committee because it included Abu Abbas! The balance of forces in the region after Iraq's defeat is now completely weighted in Israel's favour, and it is only through pressure that the latter, now ruled by the most right-wing government in the state's history, will be forced to change.

There could be a solution if the United States and Europe wanted one but their willingness will be gauged by their deeds rather than their words. If Europe is to establish a role in the Middle East, it too must exert pressure on Israel. Western Europe is a major market for Israel so it is not just the United States which can bring pressure to bear. And pressure is not only needed for the sake of the Palestinian people's right to self-determination, but because the next war in the Middle East could be even more terrible. So far only a few missiles and no chemical or nuclear arms have been used. But Syria, Pakistan and other countries will possess nuclear arms and more efficient missiles in the future. The next war in the Middle East will be far more dangerous not only for the people of the region but also for Europe and the rest of the world.

Notes
1. Thomas L Friedman, 'When War is Over: Planning for Peace and US Role in Enforcing it', *International Herald Tribune*, 21 Jan 1991
2. James Bill, *Wall Street Journal Europe*, 18-19 Jan 1991
3. Quoted by Judith Caesar, 'Rumblings in Saudi Arabia: Hear the Dissidence on Tape', *International Herald Tribune*, 11 Oct 1990. The author who is a teacher, lived in Saudi Arabia from 1987 to 1990
4. See Marc Lavergne, 'Les Jordaniens Exposés en Première Ligne', *Le Monde Diplomatique*, Jan 1991
5. *Middle East Economic Digest*, London, 18 Jan 1991
6. *International Herald Tribune*, 21 Jan 1991. The same point of view is expressed in *Wall Street Journal Europe*, 18-19 Jan 1991
7. Quoted by Gabriel Kolko, *Confronting the Third World: United States Foreign Policy, 1945-1980*, New York, Pantheon Books, 1988, pp69-70
8. Claude Julien gives a detailed account of American involvement in the coup against Mossadegh, in August 1953, in *l'Empire américain*, Paris, Grasset, 1968
9. 'The Joint Chiefs have been Preparing for Years', *International Herald Tribune*, 22 Aug 1990
10. Quoted by *International Herald Tribune*, 23 Jan 1991

Western celebration and Arab outrage

Fadia Faqir

The Gulf War rekindled Arab anger over the West's historical intervention in the region, and also revived Pan-Arabism. Fadia Faqir presents the view from the slums in the Middle East and the Palestinian refugee camps. Most Arabs are tired of being patronised by London or Washington

As Western countries celebrated victory over Iraq, millions of Arabs felt hatred and anger over what they called a 'colonial flexing of technological muscles'. The feeling of resentment which swept North African countries, Yemen, Jordan and Palestine can only be understood if it is placed in the context of imperialism, the resurgence of Islam and from the perspective of the misrepresented and abused. Many Arabs feel that their countries are ruled by Western puppets, that their economies are controlled by the International Monetary Fund and their reality is misrepresented by the Western media. The West, they argue, has consistently intervened in the developing world to further its economic and political interests, seeking to monopolise the system of representation. The conflict or quest for oil, territorial expansionism, and the drive of Western multinationals for hegemony have all been sustained by an ideological discourse in which any opposition is portrayed as ignorant, backward and evil. This was how yet another US military adventure, the so-called 'Operation Desert Storm', was justified.

During the Gulf War, anti-American feeling reached an unprecedented level in many Arab countries, and in Jordan the vast majority of the 3.1 million people actively supported Saddam Hussein. One day they even raised the equivalent of £17,000 for Iraq, in spite of having an average monthly wage of £62. And around 200,000 people signed up for the popular army of Iraq, two-thirds of whom received basic military training to defend Iraq and the 'New Jordan', including members of Parliament. For the first time in Jordan's history, the government and the nationalist, leftist and Islamic movements were united in their opposition to the West.

At that sombre moment in history, when half a million US soldiers were lined up against an Arab country, the majority of the Arab masses felt that they had to give priority to sovereignty over democracy. They felt that the sovereignty of the whole region, including a 'liberated' Kuwait, was under threat. While the West presented the conflict as a justified international campaign to stop a repressive dictator, those in the Arab world sympathising with Saddam saw the main issue as one of Arab sovereignty. If the will of the Arab world was allowed to be dictated by foreign powers, there would be no democracy, they argued, solving the dilemma by supporting the Iraqi leader — himself hardly a paragon of democracy — in his confrontation with the West. The struggle for democracy would be futile if US hegemony in the Arab world was not challenged and Arab sovereignty asserted.

US military intervention for cheap fuel and 'American values' was seen as a 'neocolonialist operation' by the Arab in the street. The US-led allies' occupation of southern Iraq provided concrete evidence that their plan was to coerce and subjugate the Arabs and brought back disturbing memories of Western involvement. Of the US intervention in Beirut in 1982-83, for example, or the return of the Queen's Royal Irish Hussars 48 years after Montgomery's defeat of Rommel, when the Desert Rats were part of an occupying colonial force. The Monties and Glubb Pashas were back, as were the Sykes and the Picots,[1] only this time they were wearing blue jeans and 'Saddam Busters' T-shirts and lacked all the romanticism of their predecessors. Arabs braced themselves for further broken promises, yet another betrayal, which would be presented in the West as a 'triumph'.

Islamic groups and parties exploited this general feeling of frustration, to stir up associations with the holy wars of the past, presenting the situation as a new crusade against Muslim Arabs. 'With or without oil', argued one Muslim fundamentalist, 'the crusaders would have invaded us for the simple fact that we are Muslims and they are Christians.' The West, so the argument went, found Islam and its active support for *jihad* (holy war), threatening and intended to suppress 'our Islamic renaissance'. In a talk in Amman just before the war, Muhammad Al-Ghazali, an Egyptian religious leader, reminded a mainly fundamentalist audience of the exploits of the Muslim Saladin who had driven the crusaders out of the Arab world. Addressing his Muslim cavalry in 1187, Saladin proclaimed that 'the Muslim army must confront all the infidels in organised battle, we must throw ourselves resolutely into the *jihad*'. Eight hundred years have passed. Yet, in the eyes of the fundamentalist *al-Franj*, the Franks, are still the same. They still want to occupy the land of Islam and free Jerusalem.

Arab nationalists had a more recent perspective. They saw the Gulf conflict as an imperialist invasion of the Arab world under US leadership, thus giving the ideology of Pan-Arabism, which had shaped the politics of the 1950s and 1960s in the Arab world and reached its zenith with the unification of Egypt and Syria in 1958, a new lease of life. Indeed, some would even argue that the ideology, which is essentially anti-imperialist, was saved by the Gulf War. While the West saw the invasion of Kuwait as a naked act of aggression against an independent, sovereign Arab state, many Arabs, brought up to believe in a single Arab homeland, have little respect for the dotted lines and borders that were arbitrarily imposed by the colonial powers. Within this context, territorial concessions are the norm and the invasion was perceived as a step towards the realisation of a united, and many hoped, democratic Arab homeland.

The conflict between the ideology of Arab nationalism — which calls for the unification and the democratisation of the Arab world and the nationalisation of its wealth and resources — and US interests in the region has never been clearer. The United States has maintained the status quo in the Middle East through military alliances and supporting regimes which have stifled internal and political dissent. Indeed the United States and the industrialised world prefer to negotiate oil prices with a corrupt ruling minority than with a democratically elected parliament. Six ruling families own 44 per cent of the world's oil. Arab nationalists believe that the West views any move towards democratisation in the Arab world as a disturbing threat to its interests in the area.

The most common view of the Gulf War can be found in the slums and Palestinian refugee camps of the Arab world. For the dwellers of the 'cities of the dead', the war was a conflict between the haves and the have-nots. The poor of Jordan, like the poor elsewhere in the Arab world, took to the streets because they hoped the conflict would lead to greater economic equality in the region. Jordan, an island of relative freedom, prosperity and stability (to borrow Malise Ruthven's words)[2] has recently become a wasteland of frustrated hopes and aspirations. The country is struggling to pay the interest on its US$8.4 billion foreign debt, 30 per cent of the population lives below the poverty line (a monthly average of US$135 per household), and one third of the population is unemployed. Inflation is running at 100 per cent and people work unlawful hours for little reward. 'We sell our merchandise and get air in return. We actually live on air,' a Jordanian salesman said. People live on very little, wearing second-hand European clothes, eating food rejected by Western countries, and living in shacks. A whole nation dreams of books and computers and of working in far-away places where people are richer and happier.

And while they wait for their dreams to come true, Jordanian people see, read and hear about Western living standards and the obscene way some oil-rich Arabs spend their money. When thousands of talented students cannot afford to continue their education, stories in the local press about birthday parties in California for Saudi cats costing thousands of dollars have a deep effect. Regardless of the truth of these reports, they feel angry and bitter. The Kuwaiti Minister to the Gulf Co-operation Council said that the Iraqis saw a paradise and decided to loot it. But it is no longer possible for a consumer paradise to exist side by side with a country with a US$60 billion foreign debt and expect peace and harmony to last. The Arab dwellers of shanty towns burnt the Stars and Stripes and the Union Jack in reaction to the economic pressure exerted on their economies by the Western creditor nations and to show their disgust at the squandering of petro-dollars.

Many Western commentators, apparently unaware of the social and political changes that have taken place in the Middle East in recent decades, aggravated the situation by talking down to Arabs, who are trying to come to terms with new realities and who feel frustrated and victimised. A Jordanian, complaining about the Western media, said: 'They come in like an army... And they know it all before they come. They don't listen; they tell us what we ought to be doing.' Most Arabs have had enough of being patronised by stern headmasters from London or Washington. The Arab countries see themselves as 30 years old or more and, like all people of that age, demand respect and understanding. Moreover, most Arabs saw the widespread support in the West for the Gulf war as hatred for Arabs and Islam. How else, they argued, can you interpret the demonisation not only of Saddam Hussein, but of his entire population? How else can one interpret the US military's sense of 'satisfaction' following the bombardment of Al-Amariya airshelter in Baghdad? How else can one interpret the silence over the attacks on Saddam's retreating military machine in which many fleeing Iraqis were killed leaving 'very, very many' bereaved families of peasant boys?

The grievances outlined in this chapter do not exist in isolation, but are interconnected and feed on each other to form a complex web of demands and aspirations across the Arab world. Unless the West overcomes its ignorance of the Arabs' history and culture, the bridges between the Arab world and the West will remain forever destroyed. The West must stop its reductionism and dehumanisation of the Arabs and Islam and place their culture in context. Otherwise the Gulf War will be followed by other catastrophes in which horrific violence is committed against an enemy presented as backward and ignorant.

Notes
1. Mark Sykes and Francois Georges-Picot, the English and French envoys, were

the architects of the inter-allied agreement of 1916 to partition the Middle East, subsequently known as the Sykes-Picot Agreement
2. Malisc Ruthven, freelance journalist specialising in Middle East affairs. Among his publications are *Islam in the World* (1984) and *A Satanic Affair: Salman Rushdie and the Rage of Islam* (1990)

2
ARAB STATES AND IDEOLOGIES

The Arab regional system and the Gulf crisis

Yezid Sayigh

The Gulf War should be seen in the light of the decline of Arab regional order and the misuse of its oil wealth. Yezid Sayigh describes the strategic impasse of the undemocratic state systems. He urges Arabs — citizens, intellectuals and officials — to work for a new civil society and open politics

For the people of the Arab world, the Iraqi invasion of Kuwait on 2 August 1990 was no less shocking than it was for the rest of the international community. Despite their immediate sense of incredulity and surprise, however, millions of Arabs had long felt that the situation in the Arab world had become intolerable and was reaching an inescapable crisis which finally arrived. Indeed, the Iraqi invasion was the dramatic culmination of a process of degradation within the Arab regional order, both within the Arab states and in terms of inter-state relations. The cataclysm in the Gulf was not therefore entirely unexpected.

Among the main determinants of Arab regional politics are strategic concerns, geographical and other material factors (for example, population size, natural resources), and the role of outside powers. But the key to understanding the dynamics governing the twin process of conflict and change in the Arab region is the interaction between the 21 countries that are official members of the League of Arab States. At the heart of this system are the governments, regimes and ruling elites formulating national policies in both the domestic and the foreign spheres. So Arab regional politics is determined by the power structure within each country that is a member of the overall inter-state system.

The basis of regional politics
The Arab countries are related by quasi-commonality of history, language, religion and culture and have economic and commercial ties and a common will for self-definition. So shared perceptions and

responses are quite natural. Most Arab nation-states as we now know them, such as Iraq, Lebanon, Libya and Kuwait, are 20th century creations and their political boundaries and separate identities were only forged during the modern colonial period, after centuries of unity or open borders. As a result, the authenticity and legitimacy of the modern nation-states have frequently been challenged.

To counter these challenges most Arab governments have, in order to ensure their continued rule, sought to disconnect their populations from the broader Arab environment, fostering local patriotism at the expense of a wider Arab identity, and strengthening the state apparatus to control the local population. As part of this process of disengagement between the state's regional and domestic activity the regimes constantly attempted to exclude the public and to prevent groups active within the state, such as the intelligentsia or technocrats, from directly influencing government policy. Decision-making has thus been concentrated almost exclusively in the hands of minority ruling elites based on family, tribal, ethnic, or sectarian lines, and almost invariably unelected. And such a concentration of power has been reinforced by the process of disengagement. The self-interested tendency of elites to establish monopoly control over the state is universal, but in the Arab case they enjoy disproportionate power and this has had a corresponding effect on the functioning and stability of the wider regional system.

The selfish system

In other words, there is a direct connection between authoritarian and undemocratic rule in individual Arab countries and their behaviour in terms of inter-state relations. This may also be true elsewhere, but again it is of special significance in the Arab case in that the fraternity of governments forming the regional state system has shown a particular interest in the maintenance of the status quo, no matter how damaging the consequences for local societies and economies.

The linkage has been most obvious in the role played by oil since the price revolution of 1973-74. This gave rise to a rentier state in which exogenous wealth — that is wealth not produced by the productive or services sectors, but available as an easily obtained surplus — has allowed Arab governments to 'bribe' major sections of the local population and alter the basis of domestic control. For many years such wealth — locally-extracted oil or transfers from other governments — enabled governments to cushion the effects of economic mismanagement or exploitation by injecting compensatory funds into the system. More to the point, by reducing government dependence on local productivity and domestic constituencies, the rentier system lessened regime accountability and made rulers less vulnerable to internal pressure for reform.

The recycling of oil wealth has also played a major role in shoring up the Arab regional system. At the public level development aid from the oil countries or remittances from nationals working there raised living standards, and helped governments to maintain social spending and thus pre-empt discontent in the 1970s and early 1980s. And, at the official level, aid from the oil-rich states allowed recipient governments to pursue inflated spending programmes that would have otherwise been impossible, including massive expenditure on the armed forces and internal security, but without major damage to the economy.

Oil wealth and official country-to-country transfers magnified the opportunities for personal self-aggrandisement and led to the development of intimate bonds of mutual interest between certain Arab rulers. This was compounded by the tendency of the recipient regimes to replicate some of the more exploitative aspects of the rentier states' economic structure. One was the monopoly on power in several Gulf states that allowed members of ruling families or clans to assert themselves as middlemen in every government contract and so make enormous profits (in some emirates this led to the direct expropriation of oil revenues). Another was the stipulation that the millions of migrant workers and expatriate professionals who have flocked to the rentier states over the last three decades could only acquire residence and employment with the 'sponsorship' of local nationals who would enjoy a majority holding as partners in business ventures. The latter have an absolute stranglehold over the 'guest' workers in terms of their legal status and profit from them without doing a day's work themselves.

Labour-donor states did not insist on guaranteed rights (equal treatment before the law) or acquired rights (permanent residence, naturalisation) for their nationals abroad, anxious not to disrupt the flow of remittances home. As a result, migrant citizens and donor governments alike experienced major uncertainty as host countries could, and did, suddenly expel whole communities of tens or hundreds of thousands of expatriates at short notice: Tunisians or Egyptians from Libya, Egyptians from Iraq, Yemenis from Saudi Arabia, and Palestinians or Jordanians from Kuwait.

This background helps explain the deepening crisis of many Arab states in the 1980s. As sources of exogenous wealth dried up with the decline in oil prices, and as the effects of chronic mismanagement or over-spending accumulated and fuelled soaring debt, governments everywhere became increasingly unable to conceal the costs and absorb internal strains.

Strategic impasse

This structural and economic crisis coincided with, and exacerbated, the strategic impasse of the Arab regional system which had already undergone major deterioration in the second half of the 1970s: the bloody civil war in Lebanon, left to suffer repeated and ever-larger Israeli incursions; the Western Sahara conflict; the Somali-Ethiopian war in the Ogaden; border wars and internal strife in North and South Yemen; Egyptian-Libyan border clashes; insurrection and Iranian intervention in Oman; armed opposition in Syria and Syrian threats to Jordan.

The next major shift in the region was triggered by the conclusion of a separate Egyptian-Israeli peace accord at Camp David in 1979. This caused a deep split in the Arab world and led to a severe tip in the balance of power with Israel, which continued to occupy all Palestinian land and the Syrian Golan Heights and started to intervene more directly and forcefully in Arab politics in the region. A year later the destabilisation of the Arab system was increased when Iraq invaded Iran. This started a debilitating war that dragged on for eight years, dominated Arab concerns and energies and paralysed the system further.

The consequences were not long in coming. Israel, having bombed Baghdad and Beirut and annexed the Golan Heights in 1981, invaded Lebanon in the summer of 1982, occupying half the country and its capital and confronting Syria in the process. Lebanon was plunged into even greater communal violence and cantonisation than before, and internal Palestinian divisions and the feud between Syria and the Palestine Liberation Organisation (PLO) became overt and violent. For its part, Jordan became increasingly worried that an expansionist Israeli government might seek to implement the slogan of 'Jordan is Palestine'.

Meanwhile, Syria allied itself with Iran in the war with Iraq. This had a 'blackmail effect' on Saudi Arabia and the smaller Gulf states, which were reportedly prompted (not for the first time, and not for the last) to pay repeated subsidies to Syria in order to moderate its foreign policy. Libya, which also supported Iran until late in the 1980-88 Gulf War, was less fortunate, having earlier sponsored an ill-fated insurrection in the southern Tunisian town of Gafsa. It thus isolated itself at a time of general Arab strategic paralysis, leaving itself exposed to a clash with American aircraft and vessels over Sirte Gulf in 1981 and to the US bombing raids in 1986. More debilitating still was its involvement in Chad which occasionally spilled over to mar Libyan-Sudanese relations. Meanwhile, the Saharan conflict continued to poison relations between Algeria and Morocco.

Wasted opportunities and demands for reform

The financial effects of the Iraq-Iran war and the decline in oil revenues from the beginning of the 1980s were pervasive throughout the Arab state system. More devastating still was the fact that the recession highlighted the chronic problems and structural weaknesses of many

Arab economies, and compounded the effects of protracted government mismanagement.

The drop in oil income reduced labour migration from population-rich Arab states to oil-rich ones and led to a fall in remittances from expatriate workers and professionals. Official aid and development loans from the oil-rich states also dropped sharply and this coincided with a general slowdown in economic growth in all Arab countries, rising indebtedness, worsening balances of trade and payments, and increasing dependence on imported food.

The 1980s, far from being the decade of economic development and integration that Arab heads of state had optimistically planned in 1980, were in fact a wasted opportunity which seemed even more drastic when the extensive human and material resources available in the region were taken into account. Such failure was due to several factors, but the main cause was the existence of a power structure in which ruling elites determined the allocation of resources in each country.

An immediate consequence of this failure was the intensification and spread of conflict throughout the Arab region. Civil war restarted with a vengeance in Sudan in 1983 (leading to a series of coups d'état); similar violence erupted in Somalia; another power struggle in South Yemen caused thousands of casualties in 1986; a further Kurdish revolt took place in Iraq; and violence became endemic along the Libyan-Chadian border. Meanwhile, civil society in Syria and Iraq was brutalised — up to 10,000 people died when Syrian troops crushed an uprising in the city of Hama in February 1982. And the Iraqi-Syrian feud again spilled over into Lebanon, with fierce battles between local proxies in 1989.

Yet the Arab regional system not only failed to respond, but even allowed much less politically complex problems to fester. Famine swept Sudan and Somalia, locusts and drought attacked Yemen and Tunisia, while Jordan and Egypt tottered on the edge of bankruptcy.

Such disarray showed the Arab world's chronic inability to control conflict at the regional level. But it also revealed how the propping up of the existing state system had ultimately led to the internalisation of strains, which reappeared in domestic instability and degeneration. The growing crisis was forcefully demonstrated by the food riots in Tunisia, Egypt, Sudan, Algeria, Jordan, and Morocco from 1984 onwards, and by the calls for political change which led to electoral reforms in Algeria and Jordan and to a relaxation of government control in Tunisia and Yemen.

Inevitable flashpoint

These developments coincided with a number of momentous events at the end of the 1980s. A harbinger was the eruption of the Palestinian *intifada* (uprising) in December 1987, which gave the Arab states an indication of grass-roots feeling. But initial hopes for a breakthrough of peace, after the PLO's decision to negotiate a settlement with Israel based on mutual recognition and partition, were dashed by Israeli intransigence, aided by a lack of resolve among the American, Western, and most Arab governments.

The stalling of the Palestinian-Israeli peace process and the start of a massive influx of Soviet Jews into Israel were seen by the Palestinians and Jordan as a direct threat to their territory and stability. At the same time Israel repeatedly demonstrated its military potential with a number of ballistic missile tests and satellite launches in 1987-90, having previously demonstrated its ability to strike with the bombing of Iraq's nuclear reactor in 1981 and the PLO's headquarters in Tunis in 1985. It had reportedly amassed awesome nuclear weapons potential. And in Spring 1990 the regional arms race finally came to the fore when Iraq and Israel exchanged threats of chemical and other non-conventional attack.

The approach of West European economic union also posed problems for Arab economies. In particular, the shadow of 1992 threatened trade and aid for the North African Arab countries (the Maghreb) as well as the future of migrant labour in the European Community. Moreover, by 1989 it was obvious that the Soviet Union's abdication as a superpower and the sweeping changes in Eastern Europe would remove one of the main pillars of support for the Arabs.

It was against this background that Kuwait and the United Arab Emirates (UAE) broke their agreed commitments to the Organisation of Petroleum Exporting Countries (Opec), exceeding oil production quotas and forcing prices down in Spring 1990. The move undermined Iraqi revenues at a critical moment, and was viewed by the Iraqi leadership (not wholly without reason) as a deliberate threat to its economic recovery, strategic influence, and domestic stability after the costly war with Iran.

The Arab state system, having already shown itself unwilling or unable to protect its weaker members — half of whom suffered chronic bloodshed, famine, or penury — now proved no more willing or able to deter the Iraqi invasion of 2 August 1990. The fact that it would be unable to respond to the invasion without outside intervention was inevitable. The state system had demonstrated its impotence, and was now paying the highest price. It may have been a shock for Westerners that the instinctive response of so many Arabs to the Gulf crisis was to rally in support of Iraq and pillory the West. But they felt they were rebelling against the regional status quo and those who had maintained political, economic, and strategic iniquities for far too long.

Altering the pattern

Outside powers, especially the United States and other leading Western nations, have exerted significant influence over Arab regional politics. Israel has also been an important actor, not just because its regional presence is a physical reality, but because its policies have had a major destabilising effect on its neighbours: it has contributed massively to the regional arms race, wreaked immense dislocation on neighbouring populations and economies, and has continued to occupy Palestinian land and disenfranchise its inhabitants for decades. Yet Israel has been allowed to remain unanswerable for its behaviour.

Nonetheless, it is incumbent on all Arabs — ordinary citizens, self-styled intellectuals or government officials — to examine their own role in creating their predicament and to bear the primary burden for getting out of it. Notions of how politics are, or should be, conducted at the domestic, regional, and international levels have been mythologised and misperceived all round and must be rethought entirely.

More specifically, the power structure and the political system on which it is based in each Arab country must undergo radical reform if the Arab people are to enjoy better lives and if inter-state relations are to be managed on a different basis. In short, political pluralism and participatory politics must replace authoritarian and oligarchic rule. Active civil society and open political institutions are the building blocks of harmonious inter-state relations and a just regional order.

There is a great danger that the post-war emphasis on ensuring regional security, possibly through structures involving Arab and/or Western partners, will again obscure the urgent need for a serious look at the region's basic problems and how they are related. For any security structure at present will be based on the very same governments that are responsible for the squandering of resources, for the accumulation of huge debts, for repression and lack of political accountability, and for arms races and open conflict. Yet all the main actors — Arab governments, Israel, and the Western nations — are poised to shore up a regional order which has caused Palestinian suffering, bloodletting in Lebanon, horrific civil war and famine in Sudan and Somalia, and the final apocalypse of a burning Kuwait and an imploding Iraq. Indeed, the conflagration caused by the Gulf War, which unleashed tremendous pent-up frustrations, is a mere indication of the price that could yet be paid.

Democracy is not a panacea, especially when the problems of the Middle East extend to fundamental issues of a strategic, economic, and environmental nature. And democratisation — whether in the Western liberal sense of the term or any other — will by no means be an easy or automatic process, and may lead to social upheaval and economic dislocation in the short term. Nonetheless, democratisation is essential, since it is only through grasping and reforging the connection between domestic power structures and the patterns of foreign-policy and inter-state behaviour that change can occur. Without democracy Arab civil society will remain victimised and mute.

*Parts of this article are abstracted from Yezid Sayigh, 'The Arab Regional System and its Politics', *International Affairs*, July 1991

Racism and Islam

Haleh Afshar

The West often views the Middle East through a racist haze. Haleh Afshar denounces the West's double standards and its distortion of Islamic realities. This only encourages a new tide of fundamentalism

The Gulf War has caused considerably more long-term damage than the burning of oil wells and the death of thousands of civilians. It was a war that was rooted in a lack of understanding on the part of the Western powers of the history, traditions and political problems of the Middle East. The war was made possible and straightforward by the West's long-standing tendency to regard the Middle East as inferior and incapable of forming its own destiny. But the likely result of this tragic episode is that the region will move towards an Islamic solution in which Western capitalism is renounced for Islamic fundamentalism.

Imperialism and images of Islam

Among other issues the Gulf War was about racism, misunderstanding and deep-rooted fears — not just the fears of the Muslim about the West and its formidable arsenal, but the fears of Westerners about Islam and its embattled revolutionary cry and fatalist disregard for life on this earth. Such fears were and still are as misguided as they are irrelevant.

Racism is partly an absence of understanding and an absence of historical perspectives. It is true that Islam conquered its empire by the sword. It would be hard to defend Islam as a religion of peace and humility. Yet the Gulf War also showed a marked divergence between theory and practice in the West's espousal of such values. If Christianity is about humility and peace, where were these qualities when George Bush responded to Iraq's request for a ceasefire with a deaf ear and an ultimatum? What happened to humility when the Americans opened fire on and 'eliminated' thousands of retreating Iraqis? Why did the US-led allies carry out their heaviest bombardment of Baghdad two hours before declaring a cessation of hostilities?

Islam is not only a religion, but a way of life and a political framework. So it becomes highly problematic if the sword is allowed to be used against the people of the book. In the West the images of the unleashed sword of Islam have been brandished more than once across the television screens, with the implicit message that death and destruction would follow if the Muslim community was not controlled. Yet if we look at the history of Islam, we find that though it conquered by the sword, it has ruled over the Middle East for the past 13 centuries by faith and not by force. It is curious how this long period of relatively untroubled rule has been forgotten or ignored by the West.

At the height of the Gulf War I often had the disagreeable experience of hearing members of the armed forces and representatives of the British government talking about the Middle East. I was hard put to recognise my own region through their language and descriptions. At a public meeting in York, I heard a Member of the European Parliament refer to 'this seething cauldron of hatred'; a York representative of the Territorial Army saw the region as 'the land of terrorism' and 'the burglars that need policing'. Both threw up their hands at a 'situation which is ghastly whichever way you look'. The reality is that less than a century of Western, Christian, 'peace-loving' imperialism has turned the Middle East into a nightmare, whereas 13 centuries of imperialism by the 'sword-waving, blood-thirsty' Muslims did not. The latter created a community of believers, *ummat*, where being a Muslim entitled people to equality before the Muslim God, a formidable deity who does not require love but demands submission, an almighty who inspires fear and imposes obedience. Islam created a unified empire, where all Muslims were regarded as part of the same nation. Muslim caliphs allowed the empire to develop its own character and the Arab conquerors became long-term settlers.

By contrast Western imperialism used its rule to drain the resources of what in the process has become the Third World. To facilitate this the people of the empire of capitalism were regarded as different, inferior, and quite unjustifiably as 'ignorant'. Racism helped the imperialists to define the Middle East as a region of resources rather than a land of people with rights and entitlements. It is therefore not surprising that the West felt no compulsion about drawing arbitrary lines across the map and creating new nation-states. It was not the Muslims who sent Bomber Harris to bomb the Iraqi tribes to force them to submit to the new borders that had been drawn up for them, separating them from their brethren. Instead of promoting unity — *ummat* — which the people of Islam — have always demanded, Western capitalism enforced divisions. It was the same bombers who came again when the Iraqis dared to transgress their British-drawn borders.

Saddam: the creation of a martyr

History is not George Bush's strongest subject, at least not Middle Eastern and Islamic history. The Americans are able to look back at Vietnam but that is as far as their historical perspective stretches. Their interest remains firmly rooted in the experience of the United States and even then they cannot remember what happened just a year or two previously in the Persian Gulf. When it was the Iranians who were suffering Iraqi mustard gas attacks, the United States and the rest of the world looked the other way. What is worse, they continued pouring into Iraq the wherewithal to make more. When leaders of the Kurdish resistance told the world of the biological attack on Halabjah, the 'civilised' world told them that they were neither the first nor the last. It merely shook its head and continued arming Iraq.

When it seemed as if, despite all this aid, the Iraqis were not winning their war against Iran, the US navy moved into the Persian Gulf. When an Iraqi Exocet missile hit a US ship, the Americans responded by bombing Iranian oil installations. When the US navy attacked an Iranian passenger plane on a scheduled flight over the Gulf, killing hundreds of civilians, the Americans decorated the ship's captain. Yet these are the people who are now posturing as the guardians of peace and justice. What peace? Whose justice?

The West could not understand why, after all the Iraqi atrocities, the Iranians opposed the new Gulf War. The militant clergy, *rohaniateh mobarez*, the cutting edge of Iranian fundamentalism, joined the fray. Their call for a massive demonstration against the war received a massive response. Astonishingly, Iranians were backing Saddam Hussein, the very man who had been condemned to death by Ayatollah Khomeini. The Iranian spiritual leader had also issued the death warrant against Salman Rushdie, but whereas Rushdie was still fearing for his life, Saddam Hussein emerged as the new hero of Islam. During the war, my phone rang non-stop. Friends in Tehran were furious. As one of them explained: 'What I hate most is that they — the allies — are making a martyr of this villain'. Saddam Hussein had already taken on the mantle of Khomeini, unperturbed by the death sentence, *fatwa*, that was still hanging over his head. The militant clergy denounced the Western imperialists and called on the public to stage protest marches:

> Once more history witnesses the disgraceful collaboration of imperialist power to demolish human rights and to pulverise Muslims, their life and their freedom.[1]

It was not that the Iranian clergy wished to back Saddam, but they were compelled to do so:

Faced with the inhuman, dictatorial invasion of the land of Muslims by the multinational imperialist forces, headed by the most bloodthirsty of hooligans, the United States of America, the least that we can do is to publicly demonstrate our disgust.[2]

The allies were the catalysts. By cutting Baghdad's water supply they made Saddam Hussein increasingly resemble the revered Shi'a hero and martyr Imam Hosein. The Shi'as, who make up nearly 96 per cent of Iranians and over 50 per cent of Iraqis, historically broke away from the majority Sunni Muslims over the issue of force versus justice. Hosein, the third Imam of the Shi'as, and the grandson of the Prophet of Islam, Hosein, rose against the unjust usurper of power, the Sunni Ummayed caliph, Yazid. The caliph's 4,000 strong army was opposed by Hosein with 72 armed men and the women and children of his family. This unequal battle, at Karbala on 10 October 680 is remembered in annual mourning ceremonies by Shi'as the world over. In every Iranian city, town and village flagellants move through the streets beating themselves in sympathy with the sufferings of Imam Hosein. Plays and pageants review the martyrdom of Hosein and his family. Yazid's strategy of barring the way to the parched descendants of the Prophet and preventing their access to water is denounced and drowned in tears of sorrow by the believers.

Thirteen centuries later it is the Sunnis who have been parched and who have been fighting an unequal battle doomed to defeat, to uphold Islamic justice. The very core of Shi'a faith and its imagery has been turned on its head in the very land where it began. The militant clergy have little choice but to declare their support: after all Shi'ism is about justice at all costs. As the militant clergy declared on the outbreak of war:

> American hands are drenched in the blood of the oppressed and the victims of its bloody murders... They have erased the homes and destroyed the lives of the Muslim people of Iraq... America has drenched the land of Muslims in the blood of innocent martyrs.[3]

Some idea of the power of this faith can be gained by the fact that it followed eight years of war in which millions of Iranians had just been wounded and killed. To this day some of my German and English students, who were not even conceived in the last World War, find it difficult to talk to each other without feelings of guilt, misunderstanding and mistrust. Yet here were the Iranians, fresh out of eight years of war, rising to the defence of their enemy. Surely such an unexpected reaction merits a moment's consideration. It is not enough to say that the enemy of my enemy is my friend — after all it was not the Americans who had fired missiles against Tehran.

But it was the Americans who created the new martyr of Islam out of yesterday's tyrannical villain. Not only did they become the source of injustice, but their every action supported Iranian suspicions that the United States was there to create havoc, kill everybody in sight and set up a new empire. Every two-bit piece of rock that was conquered in the Persian Gulf was immediately draped in the famous Stars and Stripes. The flag of victory was hauled up all over the world's television screens to mark yet another US victory. This New World Order, this imperialism, looked suspiciously like the last one and was just as unwelcome.

Double standards
As long as the West keeps its ahistorical blinkers on and goes on thinking that the Middle East is there to be divided and ruled, the region will continue to be a seething cauldron of discontent. How would a British person feel if, as an Iranian, I wreaked havoc on the Jews in Iran and then asked for the county of Hampshire to be handed over to house them permanently? Why should Muslims in general and Palestinians in particular pay for the guilt of Christians? After all Islam is heavy on obedience and submission and light on guilt. And the Palestinians had enjoyed a long history of peaceful co-existence with the Jews before the Balfour Declaration and the takeover.

If the United Nations has really woken up at last, if UN resolutions are there to be enforced, are we to look forward to the allies racing to 'liberate' the occupied West Bank and Gaza Strip? Is systematic killing by the Israeli armed forces not the same kind of killing as that of the Iraqi armed forces?

Is the beating up and even breaking of young men's bones, seen on our television screens, not quite so barbaric when the assailants are white-faced Israelis and the victims black-faced Palestinians? Or are the Palestinians just too poor to qualify for compassion or assistance? Is olive oil too inferior as oils go to cause a major environmental disaster or to warrant any kind of protection?

For the Iranian clergy, Palestine has been a major cause for concern. Already in October 1990 the government had guaranteed support for the *intifada*, recognised its organisers as official representatives of the people of Palestine and declared that Jerusalem should be seen as the base of the Palestinian government in exile.[4] The Iranian Parliament, the Majlis, appointed a special representative, Hojatoleslam Abdol Vahed Musavi Lari, to be responsible for defending the interests of Palestinians and securing funds and recognition for them. Special funds were allocated to support the children of the martyrs of the *intifada*.

The linkage of the Palestinian question with the invasion of Iraq placed the Iranian government in a difficult position, just as the sudden adoption of the mantle of Khomeini by Saddam Hussein had done. For the missile attacks on Israel were seen as cause for celebration by many supporters of the Iranian government who urged the country to join the fight against the forces of evil. But President Hojatoleslam Ali Akbar Hashemi Rafsanjani, while publicly expressing his fears about 'the excessive retaliations and ever increasing oppression and physical attacks on the Muslim people of Palestine by the Zionist regime', felt obliged to advise caution.[5] Newspaper editorials warned zealous Iranians about backing Saddam:

> Those who believe that Iran should join Iraq in the anti-American front must ask themselves this question: 'Is the Iraqi engagement against Israel a real Islamic and revolutionary battle?' If so, they must explain how Iraq has suddenly acquired this true Islamic identity? Can we trust this sudden 180-degree turn from its previous collaboration with the imperialist and Zionist forces against the Islamic republic? How can we be sure that after an intervention by Iran to support Iraq, Saddam would not make another 180-degree about turn?[6]

Their views reflected the president's determination to keep Iran out of the war, with the argument that:

> some people have been saying that we should join Saddam in his battle against imperialism... We certainly support a war with Israel, but not under the present circumstances... We would not participate in a war where either Iraq or America would be the winners...[7]

The Iranian leaders wished to remain impartial mediators and sought to formulate a peace plan, but with little success. Nevertheless they emphasised that they would respect Iraq's existing borders, support a ceasefire and demand the removal of all foreign forces from the lands of the Muslims. At the same time, of course, the Iranians continued sheltering the Iraqi dissidents, the Shi'a government in exile.

Barbarism and the rise of fundamentalism

Not only did the allies not know their enemy or the history and the politics of the Middle East, they also had no idea of what they wanted to achieve in this war. What is left if we dismiss the various interpretations that the United States needed a post-Vietnam boost, that Bush needed to be recognised as the heavy man of the West, that the arms dealers needed to parade their wares and stick 'battle hardened' stickers on their weapons? Did the allies have a long-term policy? A clue was provided in the weeks immediately after the war. The West backed Saddam Hussein in the hope that he would destroy Iran and curb the momentum of the Islamic revolution. After all, who created the fourth largest army in the world? Saddam certainly did not have all that equipment when he invaded Iran in September 1980. Now it was Syria's turn to become the policeman of the Middle East.

For those of us who have spent a lifetime opposing fundamentalism, the prospects are bleak. For fundamentalism seems to have always taken root as a result of invasions by the 'infidels'. In Egypt, Jordan, Tunisia, Morocco, Algeria and even Pakistan, Muslims are on the march to uproot *jaheliat*, barbarism, as the call to serve God rather than man, Mammon and the West is articulated in the discourse of radical Islam. Literally translated, *jaheliat* means the time of ignorance and is used by Muslims to refer to pre-Islamic times, before enlightenment. But rather than a historically specific time, it refers to any period of ignorance in the past, present or the future when Muslims lose their sense of direction and of the laws of God, and submit to the corrupt laws of people. The West is merely a glorified modern day version of *jaheliat* and imperialism the means by which it has been imposed on true Muslims. The Gulf War was therefore but one of the myriad ways that the rule of *jaheliat* is enforced on Muslims, providing yet another convincing reason why Muslims should unite and return to the true path of enlightened Islamic government.

In this there is a coincidence of interest between the Shi'as and the Sunnis. In Iran the Shi'a Iraqis have been given both a safe haven and plenty of financial support to wage their war against Saddam Hussein. Now that the war is over he has returned to his previous status of Satan and the murderous Yazid. Saddam Hussein is using the weapons he did not dare use against the allies, against his own people, the revolutionaries. Khomeini had claimed that his revolution heralded the beginning of the rule of God all over the Middle East. It suits the current regime in Iran to be able to claim that this prophecy is coming true. As a Majlis representative, Ahmad Bolukian, pointed out recently:

> We have achieved many of our goals. Now the world community realises that the Islamic Republic has been advocating a just cause. At last our enemies have realised how wrong they were and the very righteousness of our cause will enable us to export our revolution ever more widely.[8]

Of course the Iranian government is adamant in its claim that the Iraqi uprising is not fuelled by Iran and its representative at the UN went on record to deny his country's involvement. Officially, Iran's concerns are humanitarian and religious and the Iranian Security Council has repeatedly denied 'seditious' rumours saying otherwise. What Iran wants, the Council claims, is for the government of Iraq to realise that the only solution is to submit to the will and decision of its people.[9] Even if this means the fragmentation of Iraq, Iran would not like to see Kurdistan emerge as a new united country, as that would mean losing the northern provinces of Kurdistan in Iran. But the Kurds are reclaiming Kurdistan, the Shi'as are reclaiming the holy cities of the south and even Baghdad has come under threat. Fundamentalism and fragmentalism are on the march. They may not succeed this time, or the next time. But on each occasion the massacres, blood and deaths enhance the glory of martyrdom. When people believe that they no longer have anything to gain in this world, the next world becomes much more alluring. The heaven of Islam is awaiting its martyrs with open arms. All that is needed is a little desperation, a touch of bravery, and a vision of an Islamic future. The Iranian government does not need to do much. It provides a safe haven for the militants in the south, perhaps the odd weapon or two and a great deal of moral support. In the north it will offer no help, but the *peshmerga* will live up to their name. *Peshmerga*, literally translated, means the forerunner of death, the one who will die before others. The mountains of Kurdistan have never been easy to conquer and, as they have in Iran, the Kurds can continue fighting for decades.

But the fragmentation of Iraq will not come as a result of Iranian policies; it will be a direct result of the war and the subsequent bloodshed caused and watched callously by the allies. The problem has been the West's lack of understanding and of a political and historical perspective. Now it may be too late to turn the tide of fundamentalism in the Middle East.

Notes
1. *Kayhan* 20 Jan 1991
2. *Kayhan* 21 Jan 1991
3. Excerpts from the *Declaration of the Militant Clergy*, published in *Kayhan*, 19 Jan 1991
4. *Kayhan* 31 Oct 1990
5. *Kayhan* 21 Jan 1991
6. *Kayhan* 21 Jan 1991
7. *Kayhan* 26 Jan 1991
8. *Kayhan* 17 March 1991
9. *Kayhan* 17 March 1991

The Arab world and the need for cultural renewal

Khalil Hindi

The Arab world cannot take refuge either in backward nationalism or one-sided denunciation of Western exploitation. Only through thorough-going modernisation, argues Khalil Hindi, will Arab people be able to forge a new authentic politics

In the aftermath of every major Arab defeat and every cataclysmic outburst of what seems to be a collective urge for self-destruction, calls are made in the Arab world for the need to come to terms with the modern age. But while repeated with the same tedious frequency as the events which led to them, they have lost none of their immediacy and urgency, particularly in the wake of the mass destruction in Kuwait, Iraq and Kurdistan.

The gap between the Arabs and the advanced world is, undoubtedly, huge and widening all the time. Consequently, a general sense of impatience with the world seems to have seized the Arab imagination, manifesting itself in a notable lack of historicism in contemporary Arab thought and a tendency for quick fixes and historical short-cuts.

Yet such an approach has invariably proved counterproductive and pushed the Arab world deeper into the abyss. We want to short-circuit history by supporting authoritarian regimes, in the hope that they can bring unity to our countries. Instead, we end up with the prospect of Balkanisation or Lebanonisation. We want to rush history by adopting a Bismarckian solution to the problem of Arab disunity, only to end up with the crime of the occupation of Kuwait and massive fratricide and disarray; all of which are likely to prove, in the long run, more damaging to the cause of Arab unity than any imperialist machinations, real or imagined. We dream up heroes who will make history with one spectacular coup after another, only to end up with windbags of history like Saddam, who, after the debacle, did not have the courage even to resign, let alone take his own life.

Confronting myths

The contemporary capitalist world is shaped by two contradictory trends. The first is integrative, in the sense that more and more parts are embraced by the capitalist system. The second is a tendency to marginalise, pauperise and, literally crush the best part of humanity. The latter seems to have triumphed, forcing peoples like the Arabs and regions like the Middle East, save a few sparsely-populated, oil-rich sheikdoms and kingdoms, into a vicious circle of despair. But paradoxically, escaping this fate hinges on enhancing the integrative trend through determined modernisation.

Unambiguously embracing the modern age, on the other hand, is perforce a long historical process, contingent on the foundation of cultural traditions that are at variance with, in fact inimical to, those that are already prevalent. If we are to have any chance of not continuing to be trampled underfoot, we must — through complete, all-encompassing cultural renewal — embrace secularism, humanism, science, pluralism and democracy as a system. We cannot go on forever eclectically choosing one element of the modern age and shunning others; preferring one aspect but discarding another because it purportedly does not agree with our traditions or our inherited systems of values. The modern age is an integrated whole; a system that must be embraced in its totality.

Clearly, for this process to have a chance of success, it must be built on resolute confrontation, at the cultural level, with both political Islam and the semi-fascist trend within Arab nationalism. Both express a rejection of the modern world due to the pain of attempting to come to terms with alien value systems. Indeed, the current ease with which Arabs move between espousing one or the other as the road to salvation is evidence of their kinship. Further evidence is provided by Saddam's combination of appeals to Arab nationalism with calls for *jihad* (holy war). These currents may be cries of frustration, but at best they offer illusory solutions and at worst lead to horrendous self-defeats, as amply demonstrated by the Gulf War. If we Arabs are to live in the modern world rather than be consigned to its margins, we must stop retreating into the past and hankering for immediate historical glory.

Such an approach is condemned by its opponents in the Arab world as surrendering to the West. In response, one could say that, on the contrary, it is one of surrendering to the logic of human progress. Furthermore, the West is not just the West that the Arabs have known too well: the West of exploitation, destruction, mass murder, hypocrisy, treachery and perfidy. It is also the West of enlightenment, reason, science, liberalism and socialist thought.

This is the sense in which I shall use the term 'modernisation' below. A great deal has been written on the dialectic of authenticity and modernisation and many an author has agonised over whether we will lose our identity by adopting alien ways of life. But such a dichotomy is false. For pandering to calls for authenticity is likely to result in succumbing to the dominant retrograde cultural trends, rejecting the universality of human intellectual endeavour and accepting the deceitful distinction between indigenous and imported thought. And if we achieve modernisation, we will also achieve authenticity as a by-product, as no nation develops in a historical, cultural vacuum. It is only through modernisation that we will be able to transform ourselves and our traditions and make a distinctive, authentic contribution to the modern world.

Secular goals

A major obstacle to this process is the association in the Arab public's mind between modernisation and the antics of the petty rulers, particularly those of the oil-rich sheikdoms and kingdoms: embezzling public wealth to amass fabled personal riches, only to squander them on trivia like gambling abroad or building sumptuous palaces with every imaginable vulgarity, from halls of mirrors to bathrooms with gold taps. Ironically, it is these same rulers who are at the forefront of the defense of time-honoured traditions in the face of the onslaught of dangerous imported thought!

However, it is the struggle for secularisation that is likely to be the most arduous. Among the plethora of opponents of secularism the fundamentalists appear to be the most sincere. They contend that Islam is at once a religion and a state. But, in fact, throughout the Koran, Islam presents itself merely as a monotheistic religion. Moreover, the identification between religion and state, as a thesis, was put forward only relatively recently by Sayed Quttub, the founder of the Islamic Brotherhood Movement. The fact that Muslims did build Islamic states merely indicates the need to separate Islam, the history, from Islam, the religion; the first is historically conditioned and can therefore be superseded, while the second is binding for its adherents. It could also be argued that separating religion from state liberates Islam, the spiritual religion, from the burden of what Muslims did, failed to do or will do in the secular sphere.

Another school of thought seeks to reconcile Islam with enlightenment, resorting to what can only be described, in all fairness, as sophistry. It is argued that secularism is basically upholding the supremacy of reason and that since Islam is a religion of reason, it does not need an externally imported rationality. But this is a deliberate obfuscation of the central issue of detaching the religious from the secular. Indeed, Islam acknowledges the separateness of the two, but advocates of political Islam seek to subjugate the secular to the religious, while the whole point of secularism is to establish human reason and human liberty as the basis of secular activity.

Another oft-repeated argument against the validity of secularism in relation to Islam is to maintain that the former calls for the separation of church and state and that since there is no church in Islam, secularism is irrelevant. But the clergy in Islam act as custodians of the sacred, and as such the Islamic establishment constitutes a religious authority. To be sure, secularisation does not entail destroying religious authority, but calls for it to be detached from political authority and rules out the interference of one with the other. This point is especially important at a time when the rule of the religious leader (*wilayet al-faqih*) is upheld as a model of government in Iran, when calls are made throughout the Arab world for public life to be guided by Islamic regulations as interpreted by the religious experts (*ulema*) and when tyrants seek legitimacy by securing the support of religious authorities or by inventing a mythical kinship to the prophet (as Saddam had done).

A challenge to the culture of political Islam is also crucial over the increasingly degrading attitude in the Arab world towards women. It is a sad reflection of how far the retrogression has gone that 60 years after the pioneers of women's liberation in Egypt thought they had won once and for all the argument over whether women have the right to appear in public bare-faced, this issue — and whether women should be allowed to drive — is still the subject of debate today.

Laying the foundations of pluralist traditions is no less important. Here pluralism should be understood in its widest sense, not only to mean multiparty systems, but to acknowledge, in practice, the heterogeneity of the Arab world. Arabs are often portrayed in the West either as an undifferentiated mass or as a collection of tribes, sects and confessional groupings. The reality is that, while a deep cultural affinity binds Arabs together, the Arab world has been artificially divided into statelets by the imperialist powers; and while this justifiably still outrages most Arabs, the fact is that the Arab countries have, over time, become distinct entities. It is only by acknowledging such variety — both between and within the countries — that Arabs can eventually come to terms with our reality and develop forms of unity.

The challenge of self-determination

Likewise, the establishment of democratic traditions cannot be confined to democratic forms of government, but should also recognise the existence of non-Arab peoples within the Arab region and uphold their right to self-determination, including secession. This is sorely needed in the case of the long-suffering Kurdish people. The Arabs of Iraq have entered, perhaps despite the best wishes of their majority, into a power relation with the Kurds in which they have been the brutal oppressors.

It is therefore the moral duty of all Arab democrats unreservedly to defend the rights of the Kurds, including their right to their own state if they so wish. The Kurds may decide that it is in their best interests to be content with autonomy within a democratic Iraq, but this is for them to decide, not for Arabs, even if well-meaning. The adoption of such a position by a wide spectrum of Arab democratic opinion is perhaps the only way in which solidarity between two brotherly peoples can be restored.

The resolution of the Palestine question, even on terms regarded by most Palestinians as detrimental to their inalienable rights, would be a major step towards the transformation of the Arab world. The continued plight of the Palestinians, the apparent impunity and unqualified protection enjoyed by Israel, and the impetuous rejection of Palestinian peace efforts all instil a profound sense of humiliation in millions of Arabs. Why, they ask, does the world continue to be blind to our suffering and deaf to our cries for help? Why does it treat us as dispensable and with utter contempt? Is this a world worth making peace with? It is this alienation which makes Arab masses the easy prey of the bluster of adventurous buffoons and explains the unseemly spectacle of some dispirited Palestinians applauding rocket attacks on Israeli civilian areas.

The Palestine Liberation Organisation has, by advocating a two-state solution based on the establishment of a Palestinian state alongside Israel and mutual recognition, laid the basis for a historic compromise. What the Palestinians are saying is simply this: a grave historic injustice has been inflicted on the Palestinian people; it is not always possible to roll back history without causing boundless suffering on both sides; the need therefore arises for a settlement based on compromise; but for such a settlement to be just and durable in any way, it must at least satisfy the aspirations of the Palestinian people to statehood. Based on the profoundly humane desire to minimise human suffering, the Palestinian position is historically progressive on at least two counts. Firstly, it promises to heal a deep, festering wound in the collective Arab psyche, thereby facilitating Arab reconciliation with the modern world. Secondly, it promises to resolve an intensely nationalist conflict which has distorted and frustrated social progress and subjugated both Israeli and Arab to chauvinism and militarism.

Two criticisms can be anticipated in response to the analysis made in this chapter. The first is that it suffers from Orientalism. Unfortunately, the powerful and justified critique of Orientalism, pioneered by Edward Said, is occasionally misused for other purposes than those intended — to buttress an imbecile form of cultural relativism which brands any criticism of Arab society as Orientalist, or informed by Orientalism, and therefore false. It is also employed to deny the legitimacy of all foreign scholarship on the Arab world; a position which could ultimately deny the possibility of any cross-cultural interaction. It is therefore tempting to dismiss the Orientalist charge. But the argument put forward in this article does not support the idea of an immutable Arab mind that is somehow deficient and innately at odds with the modern world. On the contrary, it is based on the belief that once the creative energies of the oppressed peoples, Arabs included, are freed, they are capable of rising to the pinnacles of human progress.

The second criticism will be that confrontation with political Islam and the retrograde trend in Arab nationalism precludes the possibility of effective political action. It will surely be made by those who have been calling for nationalists, Islamicists, liberals and Marxists to form a historic alliance with which to confront the common Arab fate.

Whether such an alliance is possible or desirable is beyond the scope of this contribution. However, clear confrontation at the cultural level, as advocated here, does not rule out forming political alliances. It could even be maintained that the sharp delineation of differences provides a more stable and durable basis on which they could be built. On the other hand, cultural endeavour in the Arab world has long been afflicted by two phenomena. The first is the subservience of the overwhelming majority of the intelligentsia to the state, itself a symptom of the almost total lack of autonomy of civil society from the state. The second is that the remaining, minority section of the intelligentsia has for the most part subordinated cultural activity to immediate political considerations, thus transforming culture into ideology, that is, into the mystification of reality.

The Arab world must whole-heartedly adopt modern values and modern systems of thought and government. And this is contingent upon an unambiguous challenge, through cultural renewal, to traditions which block progress. The way forward is one of iconoclasm, puncturing myths, challenging taboos and debunking false heroes.

Ba'athist power and the future of Saddam

Marion Farouk-Sluglett and Peter Sluglett

The Ba'ath Party gained power over a backward political structure as a determined and ruthless minority. And in spite of defeat in the Gulf War, Saddam Hussein may have earned another breathing space in which to divide the opposition. But the only way forward for the country, argue Marion Farouk-Sluglett and Peter Sluglett, is the establishment of a democratic government which the Iraqi people trust

Iraq came into existence as a state as recently as 1920, as part of the peace settlement following the First World War. It was a British-mandated territory until it became independent in 1932, but it remained under strong British influence until the revolution of 1958.

Politically, Iraq is an artificial creation, formed by the unification of the three Ottoman provinces of Basra, Baghdad and Mosul; it has a population of some 18 million, divided on ethnic and sectarian lines. About a quarter of all Iraqis are Kurds, the rest Arabs; the Arabs are a Semitic people with a Semitic language (from the same family as Hebrew and Amharic), while the Kurds are Indo-Europeans speaking a language close to Persian. About five per cent of Iraqis are Christians (mostly Arabs, some Armenians and others); the rest are Muslims. Although it is difficult to establish precise figures for the various sects, roughly 55 per cent of the Muslims are Shi'as, the rest Sunnis; of the Sunnis 25 per cent are Kurds and about 15 per cent Arabs. Iraq has traditionally been governed, as it is governed now, by the Sunni Arabs of the northern cities, who form a relatively small minority of the population.

Until comparatively recent times Iraqi society was largely tribal and was thus dominated by tribal and patriarchal values. In 1947 only 35 per cent of the population lived in cities; by 1977 this trend had been reversed; over two thirds of the population, a large proportion of which are recent migrants, now live in the cities. Over the past 50 years three main avenues of upward mobility have presented themselves to Iraqis; the army, the bureaucracy and the educational system. Because of the relatively low level of industrialisation, the working class has remained quite small and has generally carried little political weight.

Although democratic in form, the political system which evolved under the British between 1920 and 1958 did not take sufficient account of the rise of new social classes, and thus new political interests and aspirations. The parliamentary system functioned after a fashion, but was corrupt — ballots were regularly rigged — and increasingly unrepresentative, and a small number of powerful figures around the monarchy effectively monopolised political power. In consequence, extra-parliamentary opposition, which was primarily left-oriented, was driven underground.

The rise of the Ba'athists

In the 1940s and 1950s clandestine politics was the preserve of the Arab nationalists, the Kurds, and above all the communists, who were the most powerful political group in Iraq and the most numerous and influential communist party in the Middle East at the time. The Ba'ath Party, which ruled Iraq for a few months in 1963 and then re-emerged in 1968 to dominate the political scene until the present time, first came to Iraq in 1953 (having been founded in Syria in 1944 as a Pan-Arab party aimed at uniting the Arab states); at the time of the 1958 revolution it had only a few hundred members.

The revolution itself began as a military coup which soon succeeded in ousting the *ancien régime*, and as there was no functioning political organisation to which the military could hand over power, had it wished, the new rulers resorted to government by decree. Partly because of the popularity and influence of the communists, the revolutionary officers, led by Abd al-Karim Qasim, did not hold elections, since the communists would almost certainly have swept the board.

After the revolution the main political struggle was between the communists and the Arab nationalists. The Arab nationalists included Nasserists and Ba'athists, and were joined by a variety of other groups, including religious Sunnis and Shi'as who feared the rise of communism, and also by supporters of the former regime. Qasim did not form a political party of his own which might have rallied or organised his supporters, and thus in February 1963 fell easy prey to a military coup, organised by Nasserists and Ba'athist officers whose principal purpose was to eliminate the left as a political force. The Ba'athists were dropped from the alliance in November, and a series of populist/statist regimes followed until the Ba'athists returned to power in July 1968.

When the Ba'ath Party took over, it had about 800 members, compared with the 25,000 members the communists had been able to mobilise in 1958. In the late 1960s and early 1970s the Ba'ath leadership built up a mass base and simultaneously organised an immense intelligence network, both civil and military, and a complex coercive apparatus of secret police to maintain itself in power. Saddam Hussein, the party's chief civilian organiser, who emerged as deputy president in 1969, was at the apex of these various networks. Gradually, membership of the Ba'ath party became a precondition for those with career ambitions, and a vast network of patronage developed. The core leadership, however, remained and still remains confined to Saddam Hussein's closest friends and associates from the late 1950s and 1960s, and to men from Takrit, the small town on the Tigris some 100 miles north of Baghdad, where he had been born in 1937.

Because of the way in which political ideologies had developed in Iraq — with a relatively low priority attached by the mass of the population to Arabism and Arab unity and a relatively high priority to social reform and economic development — the Ba'ath Party had to present itself as a socialist party and be seen to be implementing many of the policies and goals of the communists. The regime therefore developed close relations with the Soviet Union, recognised the German Democratic Republic, and, perhaps its crowning achievement, nationalised the Iraqi Petroleum Company in 1972.

Such actions helped to legitimise the Ba'athists in the eyes of those they had persecuted relentlessly over the previous decade, and the communists were eventually persuaded to join them in a national front in the summer of 1973. Of course, with hindsight — though many voiced their reservations at the time — this was the most terrible mistake, and one from which all Iraqi opposition forces should learn an important lesson, however compelling Saddam Hussein's blandishments may seem now or at any time in the future.

Problem of opposition

The Ba'athists were soon to use the newly formed coalition to present a united front against the other main opposition force, the Kurds, after their failure to negotiate a settlement with them. The Ba'ath Party and the Kurdistan Democratic Party had agreed on a plan for Kurdish autonomy within part of northern Iraq and this was scheduled to come into force in March 1974. But, as the precise location of the arrangement was never agreed upon, fighting broke out between Kurdish and government forces early in the year, with the communists giving their political support to the Ba'ath government. The Kurds were supported by the Shah of Iran, which enabled both the communists and the Ba'ath to claim that they were fighting against imperialism. Eventually, Saddam Hussein and the Shah came to an agreement in March 1975 and the Kurdish movement was momentarily crushed. By 1978, the Ba'ath Party had turned against the communists, who have been effectively proscribed since that time; the Ba'athists simply used them to consolidate themselves in power and dropped them with a vengeance when they were no longer needed.

The Shi'a opposition is a little more complicated. In 1977 the Ba'ath Party attempted, more or less for the first time on the part of any Iraqi government, to control the holy cities of Karbala and Najaf; there were riots, followed by public hangings of those judged to be responsible. This coincided with the rise of religious opposition in Iran. Khomeini himself was in Najaf for most of the 1970s and he and his followers were becoming increasingly influential. The Iraqi Da'wa Party was founded some time in the late 1960s and rallied religious Shi'as in opposition to the Ba'ath Party for its secularism and atheism and for its brutality. The Iranian revolution caused great alarm to the Iraqi leadership, which itself overestimated the appeal such a movement would have among Iraqi Shi'as; in April 1980 the leading Iraqi Shi'a opposition figure, the writer and scholar Ayatullah Baqir al-Sadr, was executed together with his sister, Bint Huda; this was accompanied by a fierce clampdown on all those alleged to be in the Da'wa party.

Although there is little hope for any long-term reconciliation within Iraq or for the security of the region unless Saddam Hussein is overthrown, it is difficult, as the terrible events of March and April 1991 have shown, to predict how this might happen. There is considerable opposition to the regime, but as well as having been prevented from mobilising politically for many years, the population has also been cowed by an all-pervading reign of terror, organised by a massive security apparatus. Equally problematic is the fact that there is no obvious alternative political force or figure behind which those who would like to see a change of government might rally.

In addition, Saddam Hussein's survival of a crushing defeat and its aftermath may well, at least in the medium term, cause people to hesitate before aligning themselves firmly against him. And many Iraqis will have understandably mixed feelings; even if they blame Saddam Hussein for having caused yet another war, they will rightly blame the West and especially the Americans for the extent to which their country has been destroyed and the senseless slaughter of their retreating armies.

The devastation wrought upon Iraq has almost paralysed the country. But it has given Saddam Hussein a breathing space to reassess his situation and has apparently allowed him to secure his own survival for the immediate future. He can probably continue to rely upon the Republican Guard and the various security services through which he has ruled for the last 22 years; in addition separate Takriti clans control three crucial military command centres in such a way that a coup attempt on the part of any one of them can be resisted by a combination of the other two. What is crucial therefore is not so much the instigation of a national insurrection but the sheer mechanics of Saddam Hussein's removal.

Events in Iraq since the ceasefire have confirmed this and have illustrated the organisational weakness of the opposition. For example there does not appear to have been any close co-ordination between the Shi'a parties and the Kurdish movement. In addition, the coalition, and particularly the United States has made great play of the notion that if the opposition forces were to succeed, Iraq would somehow disintegrate. In fact there are few grounds for supposing that this could or might happen. First, the kind of militant Shi'aism which Ayatollah Baqir al-Hakim purportedly represents has limited appeal for most Iraqi Shi'as and even the suggestion of some sort of radical Shi'a government would cause grave apprehension among all Sunnis and large numbers of Shi'as in Iraq. The main goal of most Shi'as is an end to dictatorship and representation within a democratic Iraq. As far as the Kurds are concerned, all the responsible leaders have reiterated that their goal remains autonomy for the Kurds within the framework of the present Iraqi state.

Future prospects and the challenge of democracy

Although the present situation looks exceedingly grim, it is difficult to imagine how Saddam Hussein can stay in power indefinitely. In the first place, Iraq will be isolated both regionally and internationally as long as he remains in place. Secondly, the devastation of the country's infrastructure and its key industries (particularly those associated with the oil industry) undermines the foundations of his power in terms of the regime's capacity to buy popular acquiescence if not popular support. The oil money was used to create relatively high standards of living for much of the population and its spin-offs provided lucrative opportunities for the business community until well into the 1980s. The supply of carrots is running out, and all that is left is the stick.

In July 1988 Saddam Hussein was able to project himself as victorious and took on the reconstruction of Iraq with vigour. It is clear that the present period is in no way comparable to the aftermath of the Iran-Iraq war. The leadership now finds itself virtually without funds and has lost the almost obscene Arab and international goodwill lavished upon it during and after the war with Iran. In the present circumstances, which countries or institutions are going to be prepared to lend Iraq money which the leadership would almost certainly spend on rearming itself?

It has been difficult to ascertain what is currently happening in Iraq. Millions of Kurds are stranded on or just across the borders with Iran and Turkey; hundreds of thousands of Iraqis from the south have fled into Iran in a desperate attempt to save the lives of themselves and their families. At the time of writing (late April 1991) suggestions that either or both Iran and Turkey would annex parts of Iraq seem to have disappeared from the Western media where they had been aired shortly before, although all Iraq's neighbours (and other powerful states in the region including Egypt) will no doubt consider themselves entitled to have some influence in determining the country's future. The Iraqi opposition in exile, either ignored or marginalised over the past decades, now finds itself sedulously courted by a wide variety of suitors.

There seem to be three possible future outcomes if and when Saddam Hussein is overthrown. The worst would be a government of ex-Iraqi ministers or soldiers organised and sponsored by Saudi Arabia. As the Saudis are clearly working very closely with the United States this will be recognised immediately as a clumsy attempt to impose an American solution on Iraq which would have little support within the country. One of the names mentioned as a possible future head of state is Ibrahim al-Dawud, who was Minister of Defence for two weeks in July 1968, after which he was forced to leave the country.

The second possibility is a successful military coup in which a senior general or junta of officers would take power. Although the coup leaders would almost inevitably be Ba'athists, there is no inherent reason why such a regime should be as repressive and vicious as that of Saddam Hussein. Whether such an individual or group could evoke support from the population at large is difficult to say unless he or they were to undertake to work towards the third possibility, which is the formation of a government of national reconciliation. This should include elements from all the leading political parties and interest groups in Iraq, many of which have combined in a Patriotic Alliance over the past few weeks. Although this may seem over-optimistic, the present conjuncture and the prospects which it has opened up might provide the means of restoring, or perhaps more accurately of establishing, a limited form of democracy in Iraq.

Given the complete absence of democratic institutions and the fact that over 65 per cent of Iraq's population is under 30, which means that they have no experience of anything other than Ba'athist rule, even such a minimalist demand may appear to be too optimistic. However, the only secure way forward is the installation of some kind of accountable government. If any future government is nothing more than a reflection of the regimes currently in power in neighbouring states, it will only lead to further chaos in the long run and will be unable to ensure stability and prosperity in Iraq and in the region as a whole.

The fact that the United States and Britain have been shaken out of their supineness by the international media's welcome espousal of the Kurdish cause is a hopeful sign. The United States' agreement to the general principle of establishing safe-havens or enclaves for the Kurds within Iraq would appear to indicate that the White House is at last moving away from the pathetic fallacy that Saddam Hussein's rule is better than 'anarchy', and that 'strong government' is better than 'no government'. As any political scientist knows, strong governments rule by consent, not by force; Saddam Hussein may have the monopoly of force, but if that force could be removed or neutralised, his government would fall. Two or three million people cannot be abandoned to an uncertain fate, to die of exposure while the world wrings its hands and quotes pious nostrums about non-intervention in internal affairs. Strong government in Iraq means democratic, representative government which Iraqis trust and in which they feel they have a stake and a voice.

It has been widely claimed over the last two or three decades that accountable democratic government is somehow not suitable or possible for the Third World, since its peoples are incapable of governing themselves. And such a view has been extended to the Arab world; the Iraqis or the Syrians, we are told, only understand force.

Yet it is only through the creation of some sort of accountable democratic government that violations like the invasion of Kuwait and the genocide of the Kurds can be avoided. The war and its aftermath have highlighted more than anything else the consequences of the lack of democracy, not only within Iraq but in the Arab world. The 'linkage' that must be sought is not the linkage with Palestine, which is just one aspect of the political crisis of the Middle East as a whole. If anything good has emerged from this crisis it is the growing recognition on the part of the Arabs and the West that there will be no peace, security or stability in the Middle East until the governments of the region are fully accountable to their peoples, and exercise a democratic mandate under the rule of law.

3
THE UNJUST WAR

Counting the costs of a 'simple war'

Michael Gilsenan

The real reasons for war have been mired in confusion and the United States had no strategy beyond military victory and a demonstration of power. As another arms race starts in the name of stability, it is the Arab people, writes Michael Gilsenan, who are the real losers of the war

'Saving Kuwait' was not the main aim of the war but became a secondary issue. And sanctions did not 'fail' but were discarded as a strategic option. War was the primary, not the ultimate resort. It was to lead to total victory, and total victory was to lead to American hegemony. The price of the war in human lives and suffering will be paid for years to come and will be far above even the most ghastly inflictions of the Iraqis in Kuwait. It will also be paid in the contradictions and confusions of a US policy founded on the illusion that it can dominate the Middle East and impose its own special version of 'stability'. Another instalment has been paid by the resistance movements who believed that the United States really did think that Saddam Hussein was the greatest of all evils.

Issues of war
There are strong counter-arguments to this view. Shortly before the war Samir al-Khalil wrote a powerful critique of the Iraqi regime, *Republic of Fear*. And in an equally trenchant article[1] he recently suggested that there were compelling reasons to support the US-led allies' campaign against what he called 'a criminal state'. Iraq, he said, threatened 'to destroy the modern Arab state order as we know it. Though that order may have major deficiencies, it is all we have'. The overriding issue was how to stop Saddam Hussein replacing it with something immeasurably worse. Not only was the Iraqi invasion of the greatest barbarity, but there were many Arabs who recognised that fact and did not support the Iraqis. The Egyptians knew from their own bitter experience just how brutal Saddam Hussein's regime could be and had 'no illusions'. The

Palestinians on the West Bank, on the other hand, who had not experienced Iraq in that way, had 'illusions' about Saddam; and those illusions were no basis for serious political judgement.

Samir al-Khalil suggested that what was at stake was not oil, as the Middle East Research and Information Project (Merip) editors claimed, but the far more fundamental issue of the integrity of a state and 'issues of identity and the right to be different, to be or not to be a Kuwaiti'. Saddam Hussein wanted 'to shape Arab politics and be the kingpin of the region', and he had to be stopped. Of course the United States was cynical, he went on. So what? Everyone acts out of self-interest. It was the best interests of the people of the region which mattered, not motives or intentions.

There is a strong case for many of the points which Samir al-Khalil made. But his conclusions and the price he seemed willing to pay cannot be accepted.

Of course Saddam Hussein is a criminal ruler and the integrity of the Kuwaiti state was worth defending. But it was not worth defending by whatever means and at whatever price the United States chose to employ, using the United Nations when it so felt inclined and treating the organisation with scarcely concealed contempt when it did not.

The nature of American intentions must be considered, because those intentions went far beyond the abstract issue of the virtue of restoring Kuwaiti sovereignty and safeguarding the Arabs' only semi-tolerable state order. The US project would seem to have been an overt attempt to impose 'US leadership' on the Gulf and the Arab states as a whole — a 'leadership' which may well set the Arab state order on an even less democratic course in the future. It will certainly not strengthen the 'right to be different' which Samir al-Khalil has sought to champion.

The Bush administration's strategy has subordinated the goal of 'freeing Kuwait' to a much wider-ranging, though extraordinarily ill-conceived and opportunistic, scheme to dominate the political choices of the whole region. The US conception of 'stability and order' is a narrow and muddled version of old-fashioned domination, moulded not by any 'New World Order', to use the cheap electioneering slogan, but by a view of the victory as one of the good guys over the evil empire. To fail to acknowledge this is to labour under no less of an 'illusion' than the Palestinians Samir al-Khalil castigates.

The advocates and opponents of the war should have considered three basic questions: at what cost and to whom? With what benefit and to whom? And, following on from the first two, how would the war affect the Arab societies in whose region it was to be fought?

Even assuming that Saddam was Hitler and human evil incarnate, or, less dramatically, that the Iraqi regime was akin to fascism and had to be destroyed, were the benefits of war self-evident — would it lead to the automatic assertion of international law as the Kuwaitis regained their autonomy over the grave of their oppressor? Or was the question of price and means (the two were linked of course) simply obscene because no human, social, economic or political benefit is worth such a price?

From confused goals...

Both the reasons for the war and its consequences have been mired in confusion from the beginning. As the conservative Democratic Senator Sam Nunn claimed in the fateful debate giving the president the powers he and the pro-Israeli congressmen so fervently sought, Bush failed to provide any compelling reason for committing vast numbers of US forces to the conflict.

From the first days of August 1990 President Bush even had trouble in articulating the aims of the campaign against Iraq, as many US commentators pointed out before being silenced by the need to support 'our boys' and patriotic prayer breakfasts. He fluctuated between varying combinations of the defence of Saudi Arabia, the restoration of the Kuwaiti government and state integrity, the protection of strategic US interests in the Gulf such as the oil supply, upholding freedom and international law, and the wholesale destruction of a ruler of a Middle Eastern power recently supported but now suddenly discovered to be evil. Was this simply confusion as the number of possible aims grew day by day, or a reflection of Bush's notorious verbal debility? Or was there a wider, opportunistic, yet deeply felt vision of 'American leadership of the Free World' — a vision intoxicating in its sweep but which could not be presented as compatible with the UN guidelines ostensibly legitimating the entire operation?

Let us stop to imagine a scene from August or September 1990. President Bush is taking the key decision as to whether to increase his forces in the Gulf and to switch from a defensive to an offensive posture. He knows that such a switch will almost certainly mean war. Sanctions cannot possibly 'work' in the time he can reasonably allow, in terms of keeping public opinion behind him, for half a million men to be kept ready for combat thousands of miles from home. This is a crucial point because war could only be justified to the international community if sanctions could be claimed to have 'failed'. Yet there was considerable evidence, including testimony from the CIA, that vital imports of machinery and Iraq's ability to equip itself militarily would have been hit very badly by sanctions, and the oil blockade was virtually completely successful.

Everyone knows sanctions cannot work overnight and that part of their function is to preserve space for diplomatic and political pressures. And sanctions, with proper support, would have stood a good chance of producing a negotiated settlement. But was that what President Bush wanted? Was there a much more tempting option for which many a politician would give his eye-teeth?

Day after day Defence Secretary Dick Cheney, White House Chief of Staff John Sununu, national security adviser Brent Scowcroft and, perhaps a little more cautiously, the chief of staff, general Colin Powell, backed by his airforce generals, were all saying: 'Can do Mr President. Go for it.' Technophilia was rampant and they had the weapons, smart weapons. They promised a quick and clean victory to a chief executive whose aides were strong on crisis management and poll analysis but could not see beyond such imperatives. The victory would not just be 'the liberation of Kuwait' but the far greater reward of effective US 'leadership' throughout the Middle East. Bush, Cheney and Scowcroft are products of the Cold War. The 1950s discourse of good and evil forces, of worldwide pacts, bases and influence comes naturally to them.

...to a 'simple' war

Imagine the insistent voices: 'Here is a window of opportunity, Mr President, take it. Iran is weak. Egypt is ours. Syria hates Iraq. Turkey is in our pocket. The Gulf states will do exactly as they are told. The Saudis will have no choice. Israel will love it. We will control the flow of oil. The Cold War is over and we have won. But we have a major economic crisis; the Europeans and Japanese are serious competitors. Even some Americans say we are no longer a world power, that we are in decline; the Gulf War will change that. The Brits will assert their Atlanticist identity — Thatcher loves the idea and it will be a blow against the EC. The Europeans will do what they are told and come on board. Our wishes for a strong and interventionist Nato will be strengthened in this difficult period after the demise of the Warsaw Pact. We can use the UN and have bases and a permanent presence in the Middle East if we wish. Cut them off and kill them. Take it, Mr President.'

War simplifies — an attractive view when dressed in more sophisticated and solid analytical clothes. This was a 'just cause' which promised later electoral success, provided an all-out assault on the enemy could ensure a swift victory. That was never in doubt, because no one could imagine that 'we' were not going to 'win'. But no one ever analysed exactly what 'winning' would mean in the real world of the Middle East, apart from the political and economic leverage it would give the United States.

That explains the plethora of reasons which President Bush found for the enterprise. What he could not do, of course, was articulate his true reasons of state which made perfect sense in the US administration context and obeyed all the rules of realpolitik, including the rule that you should have God on your side. The destruction of the Ba'athist regime, of Iraq's armed services, of its manufacturing and industrial sectors, infrastructure, energy supply and its ability to sustain any normal level of social life could all go ahead 'in order to restore the sovereignty of Kuwait'.

Only two costs would seem to have received systematic consideration — the number of body bags and the amount of money. If the airforce chiefs could guarantee a quick kill and low casualties, both President and Pentagon would be able to avoid the 'Vietnam nightmare', of losing public support in a long drawn-out struggle far from home. They gave that guarantee. The problem of money was James Baker's responsibility. If he could get contributions from Japan, the Germans, and above all, the rich Arab states, the war would not only more than pay for itself, but also give an unambiguous demonstration to the world of who was in charge of the New World Order. Baker was able and did so fast, giving a brilliant object lesson in the art of applying intense pressure. And just as the UN had been sewn up in a masterly fashion in the early stages, the Secretary of State now gathered the necessary billions. The US budget has not been harmed, and the Republicans have been able to fight off talk of a 'peace dividend' and relaunch some of their cherished defence projects such as the costly B-2 warplane.

Monopoly of power, monopoly of gain

The administration demonstrated speed and foresight in recognising that those who have a monopoly on the means of destruction can translate that into a monopoly of gain. It realised long before anyone else that there was another war to be fought — what *Le Monde* called in a front page headline 'La bataille des plans de paix'. The newspaper's headline on the financial page was more precise: 'La victoire des industriels américains'.[2] This was a war against America's allies, proudly led by Britain, for vast reconstruction contracts in Kuwait (and no doubt, in time, in Baghdad itself). By 'vast' we mean estimates of between US$50 billion and US$150 billion. There are fat profit margins for Caterpillar, Bechtel, Fluor Daniel, Brown and Root and Foster Wheeler. Readers of the *Financial Times* will have noted the reports on the formation of major powerful consortia.

They will also certainly have noticed the squeeze on non-US business. As the *Financial Times* noted in a report headlined 'US and UK groups battle it out for contracts': 'British engineers say US project managers traditionally prefer to operate with other US companies.'[3] It also reported that US manufacturers were urging the Bush administration to 'ease the US domestic recession by taking more vigorous steps to promote exports'. The link was clear. One could only wish luck to the chairmen of Morgan Grenfell, Amec, John Brown Engineering, the Crown Agents, Department of Trade and Industry officials, as they desperately hustled the Kuwaiti government-in-exile in Taif, picking over the bones left by their voracious US allies. Both the United States and Britain made explicit use of their military contributions in the ferocious bargaining over business as the air attacks continued. The war has brought tremendous financial, as well as political, rewards for the United States.

The stakes in the arms trade are scarcely less hallucinatorily vast. No one, least of all James Baker or Douglas Hurd, is proposing stopping the trade in so-called 'conventional' weapons, in spite of all the piety about nuclear, biological and chemical arms. One of the United States' first reactions to the end of the war was to talk of the Gulf states' need for 'additional security'. The West and the Soviet Union have for years, with the enthusiastic help of local rulers, turned the entire Middle East into a region with catastrophically high expenditure on arms. Britain has been involved in a 'sale of the century' with the Saudis, reportedly worth some £20 billion over 20 years. Iraq is said to have spent around 25 per cent of gross domestic product on arms, and others are not far behind. Now the West will have an almost monopoly position, provided that the Chinese, Brazilians and local arms industries do not take too much of the trade. These policies, socially and economically crippling for Arab societies, will be enthusiastically continued in another arms race started in the name of the very regional 'stability' they will necessarily undermine.

One day a specialist will track the capital flows associated with the whole episode from day one. Israel presented a bill-cum-claim for US$13 billion; the Turks have been more than vigilant and needed compensation; Egypt was quickly forgiven its US$7 billion arms debt but needed more; Syria had funds unblocked by the EC and found a new 'respectability' over its role in Lebanon; the United States received its war subsidies; and the Soviet Union was tied to the United States by its need for help. The air has been thick with pay-offs and promises, massive promises, each with its own complex politics contradicting most or all of the rest.

To find out who is paying the price and who is benefiting, *cherchez la monnaie*. What are the losses and benefits for 'the Arabs' (a term which is often used to include the Iranians, and sometimes the Turks)? We know that Western arms, engineering and construction industries have gained. We know the United States' hoped-for political goals. We know oil-rich regimes have bought their safety and that others have gained a dubious new credibility in Western eyes. There must be some benefits to the Arab peoples themselves.

But are there? Kuwait has been shattered by the Iraqi regime. Iraq has been terribly battered: its infrastructure is devastated; major cities have been bombarded with incredible amounts of ordnance, which turn out mostly to have been 'dumb' bombs rather than 'smart' bombs that television would have us admire — a distinction between military and civilian targets would seem, in practice, to have been barely been made. Jordan has been crippled. The expulsion of 700,000 Yemenis from Saudi Arabia has devastated the south Arabian economy. The Palestinians have been hammered. The human and environmental costs have been terrifying. Yet despite the effects of the war 'the Arabs' seem even less of a real presence than before. The abyss between 'us and them' has become even greater, whether or not they are 'on our side'. They vanished in a sandstorm of media blitzes on Baghdad which technologised the war — with the false immediacy of 'real time' and the pseudo-actuality of 'live from Amman Riyadh Dahran' — and demonised Saddam Hussein.

'They' are more of an absence and puzzle than ever. The wheeling and dealing of regimes was not thought very mysterious. What was striking was the bafflement expressed by many in the West (of all level of education and experience) at the various Arab reactions to the invasion and occupation of Iraq, and the bombing of a celebrated capital, Baghdad, as well as an important city, Basra. How many 30-second sound bites were spent during the war treating outrage in the streets of Arab cities as inexplicable? Or apparent Iraqi solidarity in the face of aerial attack as unexpected or astonishing? How often was a strong sense of honour and face evoked as something peculiarly Arab, as if such a concept were alien to American, British or French politics?

Perhaps what is so bewildering about 'the Arabs', it would paradoxically seem, is that this undifferentiated 'they' are in fact behaving as 'we' might be expected to behave if 'we' were in such a situation. But because they are regarded as utterly alien and not us — the barbarians outside the city — and because we, the powerful, cannot imagine being the victims of such a war, their reality is perceived as incomprehensible. I have been repeatedly asked for a deep cultural explanation of profound differences between 'us and them' during and after the war. And as that dubious creature — a Middle Eastern specialist — I have a vested interest in talking about historical and sociological specificities. They certainly exist. But almost invariably an answer does not seem to require any special insight into unique cultural peculiarities, but quite simply a political interpretation of the situation.

Arab culture: whose myths?

'Saddam Hussein' in 'Baghdad', attacked by the world's greatest power and its allies, became a symbolic vessel into which unlimited grievances and frustrations could be poured. Denied political and civil rights in most of the Arab world by various undemocratic regimes, many people used Saddam as a confused but powerful instrument with which to criticise their own rulers, never mind the powers they associated with colonial rule and domination of the contemporary world. Is that incomprehensible, even when we, and many Arabs — when the sounds of war were not deafening them — recognised the vileness of Saddam's regime and the total horror of the invasion and occupation of Kuwait? Arabs were informed in majestic neo-colonial tones and with disingenuous grace by the British foreign secretary that they 'have a part to play' in the settlement of their own affairs — an assertion that brought a wintry smile to the lips of those who could remember similar assurances from other foreign secretaries. Is the Arabs' sense of humiliation so difficult to grasp? Is it not in fact much more extraordinary that a British minister should find such a statement positively generous and should have no sense of its presumption? The Syrian foreign minister who, after meeting Douglas Hurd, evoked the Sykes-Picot agreement of 1916 in which the British and the French secretly carved up the Middle East between them (later using the League of Nations to give them so-called mandates as a cover), was not making some arcane and irrelevant allusion. As much as a knowledge of 'Arab culture' it is a minimum of historical awareness and a willingness to confront our own past which are needed to teach us that.

Any proportionality between the crime — a real and appalling crime — and the punishment was lost during the Gulf War. And the agenda currently being imposed by the Americans and their subordinates does not address the issues identified by Samir al-Khalil. Despite the deeply disturbed and complex world of our calculations, we can see that the price exacted from the Arab people is neither right nor just.

Not only that but it transpires that 'the allies' were quite willing to stand back and allow the Republican Guard — that bastion of the Hitler-like Saddam Hussein which, we were told a thousand times, had to be destroyed in order to destroy the evil genius himself — to move south on the offensive against the resistance. Could Stalin's decision to refuse to support the Warsaw uprising and allow the Nazis to exterminate the resistance fighters have been any more cynical? And are we now to believe that Saddam Hussein is after all a lesser evil than the different opposition groups, just because the Americans have now discovered they prefer 'order' under a battered dictator to the alternatives? Is this protecting the best state system the Arabs could have?

The lessons being given by the United States are clear. There are to be no more people's wars against dominant world powers. There is only one such power and it will not tolerate opposition, whether in Grenada, Panama or Iraq. The destruction of the stranded fleeing columns was a blood sacrifice intended both to exorcise American shame after Vietnam, and as a demonstration of raw power and potency. As General John R Galvin, supreme allied commander in Europe, has said, Nato's future role means 'that in a crisis you don't sit on your hands but you do military things that will bring greater stabilisation to the area of crisis.'[4]

'Military things.' The old recipe. The grand illusion.

Notes
1. *Merip 168*, Jan-Feb 1991, pp14-17
2. *Le Monde* 8 Feb 1991
3. *Financial Times* 11 Feb 1991
4. *International Herald Tribune*, 25 Feb 1991

Arab losses, First World gains

Tim Niblock

The real winner of the Gulf War is the developed world, while the heaviest costs are borne by those who suffered. Tim Niblock counts the costs of the devastation. The cause of Arab unity, he concludes, must be revived to save the region

Identifying who wins a war is rarely the same as identifying who gains from it. And in the contemporary world, the economic repercussions of military action are particularly complex and far-reaching. The Gulf War was won by a coalition of powers, acting with the authorisation of the United Nations Security Council and under the leadership of the United States. Nine Arab countries gave significant political support and contributed military contingents for the battle: the six countries of the Gulf Co-operation Council, together with Egypt, Syria and Morocco. Six other Third World countries and five European countries also sent military contingents. They were all part of the winning coalition against the loser, Iraq.

Yet the countries which have gained or will gain from the war is a very different matter. The war has led to massive changes in the balance of economic resources and potential between the core of the developed capitalist world and part of the Third World. The former constitutes the real 'winning coalition', leaving the Arab countries (whatever stand they took in the actual conflict) the losers. The United States and its Western allies led the campaign to uphold the principles of international law; in the process they will reap substantial financial benefits. It is the Arab countries, however, which have footed most of the bill for the defence of such principles, and have suffered the destructive effects of the operations undertaken.

The Arab losses

Each Arab country has suffered its own particular form of losses as a result of the war. There have been seven different kinds of material losses: the destruction of resources (with the consequent need for expenditure on reconstruction); financial contributions to other countries; the disruption or blockade of trade; the reduction of remittances from nationals working abroad; the reduction in aid and assistance; the provision of humanitarian assistance and support for displaced residents of Kuwait; and additional defence expenditure.

Iraq

The outcome of the war for Iraq was clearly ugly. Yet the full scale of Iraq's losses should be emphasised. The clearest picture of the scale of the country's destruction has been a report written by Martti Ahtisaari, the UN under-secretary-general, in the immediate aftermath of the war. Compiled after Ahtisaari had spent the week of March 10-17 in Baghdad, the report states that the war had:

> wrought near-apocalyptic results upon the economic infrastructure of what had been, until January 1991, a rather highly urbanised and mechanised society. Now, most modern means of life support have been destroyed or rendered tenuous. Iraq has, for some time to come, been relegated to a pre-industrial age, but with all the disabilities of post-industrial dependency on an intensive use of energy and technology.

The report makes clear that a large part of Iraq's infrastructure has been destroyed: its telecommunications and power generation and supply systems almost entirely, and much of its transport system, industry, and water and sewage network. The devastation seems absolute: all previously viable sources of fuel and power (apart from a limited number of mobile generators) and modern means of communications are defunct; most employees are simply unable to go to work; about 90 per cent of industrial workers have been reduced to inactivity and are no longer being paid; government departments have only marginal attendance; all electrically-operated installations have ceased to function as a result of the destruction of power plants, oil refineries, main oil storage facilities and water-related chemical plants; and the banking system has in large measure closed down. The role of energy, the report points out, is particularly important in Iraq because of its level of urbanisation (about 72 per cent of the population lives in towns), its industrialised nature and its long and hot summers:

> Minimum survival level to undertake humanitarian activities would require approximately 25 per cent of pre-war civilian domestic fuel consumption. Its absence, given the proximate onset of hot weather conditions, may have calamitous consequences for food, water supply and for sanitation; and therefore of health conditions.

The impact of the devastation on everyday life, and on every sphere of economic activity, makes clear the scale of the reconstruction which will be necessary. The sole laboratory producing veterinary vaccines has been destroyed in raids which also destroyed all existing stocks of these vaccines and there is now no way of combatting livestock diseases. The main seed warehouses have been destroyed, together with all stocks of vegetable and potato seeds. Irrigation and drainage systems for agriculture have been disrupted. The supply of water in Baghdad has sunk to less than 10 per cent of what it was before the war, with the destruction of many of the pumping stations. The sewage-treatment facilities in Baghdad are now out of action (due to the destruction of the power stations), and untreated sewage is being pumped directly into the river (from which many of the towns of Iraq draw their drinking water). All internal and external telephone systems have been destroyed (with the exception of a limited local exchange in one town). Information in today's Iraq, the report says, can only be exchanged by person-to-person contact.

Further damage not mentioned in Ahtisaari's report has been caused by Iraq's own action: the degradation of agriculture through the setting alight of Kuwait's oil wells. Paradoxically, it is agricultural production in Iraq which may suffer most from this man-made disaster, as soot deposits and sulphur contaminants from acid rain will damage soil fertility in southern Iraq, where excessive salinity has long been a problem.

The damage to Iraq's military installations, equipment and armaments has, of course, also been substantial. An estimated 3,500 out of 4,200 tanks were destroyed, as were 2,000 out of 3,000 artillery pieces, and 2,000 out of 2,700 armoured troop carriers.

Since the imposition of the UN sanctions in August 1990, Iraq has lost practically all of its earnings from oil exports — previously running at about US$80 million per day. It will now need to make compensation payments through the United Nations Committee. These, once Iraqi oil exports restart, have been set at 30 per cent of export proceeds, which at the previous level of production and at current prices, would come to some US$9 billion per annum.

Some have suggested that the material losses to Iraq may be in the region of US$110 billion. Estimates of this nature, however, have little value: not enough accurate information is available. The cost of the war in human lives is similarly difficult to calculate with any precision. Probably at least 100,000 lives were lost in the war itself, and at least half that number in the tragedies immediately after the war (through to mid-April): the uprisings in the Kurdish areas and in southern Iraq, the disturbances in some northern and central Iraqi cities, and the deteriorating health, social and security conditions throughout the country.

Saudi Arabia

A significant part of the costs incurred by the coalition confronting Iraq have been borne by Saudi Arabia, rivalled only by the exiled government of Kuwait as the main financier of the war.

Two main kinds of expenditure have been involved: payments to the United States and other countries which supplied military contingents to the coalition, to cover the costs of deployment; and payments to states whose political support was needed to create and maintain the coalition against Iraq. Some of the payments were in cash and some in kind (the latter mainly involved Saudi Arabia covering the costs of fuel and provisions for troops on Saudi territory). Rather less substantial was the expenditure needed for the mobilisation of Saudi Arabia's own defence forces (excluding new weapons orders, which were of longer-term significance).

Total pledges to coalition members who supplied military contingents came to about US$22 billion (of which the United States gained US$17 billion). Pledges to other countries for political support and to alleviate problems arising from the confrontation with Iraq came to about US$7 billion. No estimates were available for Saudi Arabia's own mobilisation expenses.

Two other types of expenditure have arisen for Saudi Arabia. The first is for the repair of damage inflicted by the Iraqi military: the destruction of industrial plants in Khafji, the oil pollution along the Saudi coast, and the rather light damage caused by Scud missiles. The costs here are likely to be limited to between US$1 and US$2 billion. The second is more substantial: the order of new weaponry for the Saudi armed forces. In September 1990, a weapons order for US$20 billion was submitted to the United States for the purchase of F-15 planes, Apache anti-tank missiles, Patriot missiles, 400 M1-A1 tanks, and 500 Bradley armoured fighting vehicles. A further order worth US$3 billion was submitted in March 1991, mostly for Awacs planes.

Saudi Arabia's total expenditure arising in the crisis over Kuwait is therefore likely to be over US$50 billion. The rise in oil prices and Saudi oil production which occurred soon after the invasion of Kuwait brought Saudi Arabia some gain. This, however, was limited relative to the added expenditure. Total Saudi oil revenues in 1990 did not exceed US$30 billion, and the country's overseas holdings in mid-1990 stood at rather less than US$50 billion.

Kuwait

Inevitably Kuwait has been a major loser and will continue to incur expenditure for the country's reconstruction. The material losses include payments to coalition members to defray the costs of their military operations, the destruction of oil stocks and reserves (below and above ground), the costs of re-equipping and re-forming the Kuwaiti armed forces, the damage to the environment from oil fires and oil spillage, and the costs of repairing Kuwait's oil production facilities, infrastructure, and housing stock. The loss of oil revenues has not been included, as oil kept in the ground can be sold later.

The Kuwait government-in-exile's pledges to coalition members came to about US$19 billion, of which US$15 billion was for the United States and about US$1 billion for the United Kingdom. The initial phase of reconstruction is expected to cost about US$25 billion, but the total may ultimately reach US$50 billion. No reliable estimates are available for the costs of rearmament; possibly between US$10-20 billion would be needed. During the first two months after Kuwait's oil wells were set alight, oil worth some US$100 million a day (according to figures provided by the Kuwaiti government) was lost. Assuming the steady capping of wells over a one-year period, about US$20 billion worth of oil may have been destroyed.

The material costs of the Iraqi invasion and the war, therefore, have come to between US$70 billion and US$100 billion. Kuwait's total overseas holdings, collected assiduously over the previous 30 years to provide an income when oil ran out, stood in mid-1990 at about US$110 billion. Compensation payments from Iraq may bring in US$4 billion annually, but the political practicality of the compensation arrangements (whether in the short term, when Iraq's own needs will be critical, or in the long term, when political conditions may have changed) is debatable.

The human costs have also been significant. Although the loss of life among Kuwaitis seems to have been considerably less than originally supposed (probably not more than 1,000 and perhaps even less), the pollution of Kuwait's atmosphere and terrain may have long-lasting medical effects.

The Palestinians

Before the Iraqi invasion Kuwait had hosted the largest expatriate Palestinian community in the world — Jordan excepted. Ever since the Palestinian community in Lebanon had come under pressure in the mid-1970s, the community in Kuwait had emerged as a focus among Palestinians. Of the 700,000 Palestinians in the Gulf countries (in a world community of six million) 420,000 were in Kuwait. They made up 20 per cent of the total population of Kuwait, which stood at 2.2 million before the invasion.

The Palestinians have suffered losses of residence, of property and of access to finance. By the end of March 1991, only 120,000 Palestinians remained in the country. Kuwaiti government policy after the invasion was that the exit of the remaining Palestinians should be 'processed legally'. Palestinians in Saudi Arabia and other Gulf states were also under pressure to leave. The Palestinian economist George Abed has estimated that the resources and assets held by Palestinians in Kuwait, and now written off, as worth about US$8 billion.

Income from Palestinians in Kuwait underpinned the standard of living of Palestinians in the occupied territories. George Abed has shown that more than half of the US$700 million which flowed into the West Bank and Gaza in 1989-90 emanated from Gulf Palestinians. Without this support, per capita income on the West Bank and Gaza will fall by between 15 and 20 per cent to US$800 per annum — a mere half of what it was before the *intifada* began, and just one tenth of the annual income of Israelis.

The financial support of Gulf governments for Palestinian organisations has also been lost. Before the invasion of Kuwait, one tenth of the salary of every Palestinian employed in Kuwait was deducted and sent to the treasury of the Palestine Liberation Organisation — from which it was used to support the social and educational services provided by the PLO to Palestinians in different Arab countries. Regular government grants have been lost.

The Palestinian losses have so far been contained within the Arab world and no outflow of resources from the region has occurred. But it is difficult to predict the effects of further Palestinian dispossession in the long term.

Other Arab States
The war has similarly affected the four partners of Kuwait and Saudi Arabia in the Gulf Co-operation Council. Bahrain, Qatar, the United Arab Emirates and Oman all made contributions to the coalition countries in cash and in kind. All despatched military contingents to Saudi Arabia and all bore the costs of providing housing and support for Kuwaitis who took refuge in their territories. While the overall costs remain unclear, some elements are known. The UAE, whose contribution was described by US Congressman Lee Aspin (chairman of the House Armed Services Committee) as 'inadequate', pledged US$4 billion to the United States alone, equivalent to US$10,000 for every UAE citizen.

The poorer countries in the Arab world have lost through the reduction of remittances from nationals employed in Gulf countries, the disruption of trade, and in some cases the reduction or termination of aid. Jordan, Yemen and Sudan have been particularly affected. Jordan's gross domestic product has declined by 37 per cent since July 1990; meanwhile the country has had to cope with a massive influx of refugees, as well as of its own citizens returning from the Gulf.

Egypt would appear to be the only Arab country which may have gained. Of the US$50 billion which Egypt owed to foreign debtors in July 1990, a total of US$15 billion has been forgiven — seven billion in military debt to the United States, and the remainder debts to the governments of Gulf states. Whether this will balance out Egypt's losses, however, is not clear: remittances from Egyptian workers in the Gulf have declined sharply since the invasion of Kuwait, as have earnings from tourism. The loss from these two items in the first three months after the invasion of Kuwait has been put at US$5 billion. Nonetheless, the close relationship forged between the Egyptian and Gulf state governments is likely to be of some long-term benefit to Egypt.

Syria has gained extra financial support (some US$2 billion) from Saudi Arabia for its support for the coalition, but it seems unlikely that this will balance the losses. Libya and Algeria appear to have lost little and gained little.

First World gains

In comparison with wars in the 19th and 20th centuries, the Gulf War has one unusual characteristic. Those who orchestrated and carried out the military operations (on the side of the coalition) have borne little, if any, of the expense.

Estimates of the cost of US military operations remain confused, even within the US administration. The congressional Budget Office suggested in March (when hostilities had ceased) that initial estimates of US$60 billion were excessive and scaled these down to about US$42.5 billion. Early in April, a report from the House armed services committee put the expenditure — surprisingly — at US$70.5 billion.

The pledges made to cover US expenses are clearer-cut. They total some US$54 billion, of which Saudi Arabia is contributing US$17 billion, Kuwait US$15 billion, Japan US$9 billion, Germany US$9 billion, and the UAE US$4 billion. The pledges will be honoured. Failure to do so carries sanctions: Congress has determined that non-payers will be debarred from further purchases of US weaponry. Whichever estimate of US expenditure on the war proves correct, the United States has undergone no substantial loss (relative to the losses of Arab countries) and may even have made a profit.

Britain's position is similar. The total cost of Britain's military involvement now seems unlikely to have exceeded £3 billion and may have been substantially less. Pledges of support come to about £1.5 billion, mainly from Kuwait (£660 million), Saudi Arabia (£300 million), Germany (£295 million), and the UAE (£250 million).

The costs of the military operations, however, represent only one part of the balance of gain and loss to First World countries. While some First World countries (Japan and Germany in particular) may have had to bear a significant part of the financial burden, all the developed capitalist world seems destined to gain from the restructuring of relations with the Arab countries which will now ensue.

Three aspects of this re-structuring require particular emphasis, relating to the resolution of problems which had previously frustrated the aims of the developed capitalist countries in the Middle East.

The first concerns the recycling of petro-dollars. Since the early 1970s, the developed capitalist countries have faced a dilemma: how to attract the huge revenues earned from oil production back into the First World economies without Arab investors gaining control of large swathes of Western industry. The problem threatened to become increasingly acute once the Arab oil-producing states had completed the construction of basic social and economic infrastructures. Revenues which had been absorbed by contracts with Western companies, for the creation of the infrastructures, would be freed for investment in Europe and the United States. Kuwait's acquisition of a major share-holding in British Petroleum in 1989 stirred the concern.

The Gulf War has resolved this Western dilemma. At least for the next five years, Arab oil revenues will need to be devoted largely to reconstruction and rearmament. Huge contracts for reconstruction are already on offer. Some arms shopping lists have been presented and others are being prepared.

The second problem concerns oil-pricing. The ability of oil-producing countries (when conditions are right) to raise oil prices abruptly has threatened the stability of First World economies. The problem was expected to intensify in the 1990s: the production of oil outside of the Gulf area will decline, leaving the industrialised world more acutely dependent on Gulf oil than ever.

This dilemma too has been resolved. On the one hand, the Gulf states will be in no position to restrict oil production; their need for revenue, so as to recoup their losses, will be too great. And on the other, they will lack the political strength needed to confront First World interests. The stand taken by the Organisation of Petroleum Exporting Countries in the early 1970s was not just the result of the demand for oil exceeding supply, but also of political factors: the British withdrawal from the Gulf (completed in 1971), the changes of government in Libya (1969) and Iraq (1968), the assertive role sought by the Shah, and the strengthening of the Saudi state under Faisal. The events of 1990-91 have emphasised and reinforced the strategic dependency of the Gulf states.

The third problem, from a Western perspective, also relates to oil. The Palestine issue has consistently affected the relationship between the

Gulf states and the Western powers, threatening the continuity of oil supplies. The zeal with which Gulf governments press this issue will diminish. The governments are in a weaker position than before to exert pressure and their dissatisfaction with PLO statements following the invasion may sap whatever resolve they retain.

The need for a regional framework

The cause of Arab unity has long since been seen as outmoded. Within the casing of Arab nationalist ideology it has been used to justify dictatorship and aggression. In the wake of the war, the basis for Arab unity has never seemed so frail. Yet the events of 1990-91 point to the continued relevance of conceptions which had sunk to the level of empty rhetoric and the need for a measure of regional unity has again been revealed.

The system of states imposed on the eastern Arab world in the wake of the First World War has been divided since its inception and external powers have gained as a result. The scale of Arab loss and First World gain today is more massive than before, but the pattern is not new. Indeed the divisions are not accidental or incidental, but structural. The interests, identities and objectives of the states of the eastern Arab world are interlinked and the actions of one state have a crucial effect on its neighbours. Labour supply and demand, communications routes, strategic needs, water supply, communal and regional identities, the Palestinian issue, the optimum means of exploiting resources — all constitute fields of necessary interaction.

An overriding regional framework is needed within which these interests can be reconciled, made compatible and co-ordinated. But the institution of a new framework must be based on democratic accountability if they are to have a strong claim to legitimacy. Without such a framework, renewed conflict will arise with the same process of regional loss and external gain.

The United States and Palestine: Avoiding the issue

Abbas Shiblak

The Palestine Liberation Organisation worked for a political solution to the invasion of Kuwait and the West's insistence on war has condemned the Palestinians to further persecution. Abbas Shiblak, imprisoned by the British government during the war, outlines the Palestinian dilemma and the short-sighted nature of US goals

The Palestinians' stance was widely seen in the West as supportive of Saddam Hussein. But this was the arbitrary and over-simplified interpretation placed on it by the US administration which suddenly divided the world into two camps: those who were pro-Saddam and those who were anti-Saddam. It was a return to the early 50s when one often heard the blunt American ultimatum: you are either fighting with us or you are against us. The US administration became the custodian of the world's morality. Small countries like Tunisia and Jordan, with a long-standing pro-Western stance, were penalised for not joining the US-led coalition in the Gulf.

The Palestinian position
The PLO's official position upheld the principle of the withdrawal of Iraqi forces from Kuwait, the avoidance of war and foreign intervention, and the quest for a peaceful solution —primarily an Arab one. Yasser Arafat endeavoured through shuttle-diplomacy to find a solution to the crisis. The Palestinian plan presented to the Arab summit on 10 August 1990 proposed the withdrawal of Iraqi troops from Kuwait, their replacement with Arab forces and a negotiated solution within the framework of the Arab League, dealing with the issues of Iraqi debts to Kuwait and the borders. The two Kuwaiti islands would remain under Kuwaiti sovereignty but under a 'lend-lease' formula they would remain at the disposal of Iraq so that Baghdad could gain access to the sea. However the US military build-up and the pressure exerted by Washington, mainly on the Saudis and the Egyptians, plunged the Arab

summit meeting into crisis. All the proposals for an Arab solution to the crisis, including the Palestinian one, were rejected. In fact the early American intervention altered the debate in the Arab world from concern over the invasion of Kuwait to what seemed to be a far more destructive threat. Many felt strongly that the main Arab objective should be to give diplomacy a chance and avoid a devastating war over which the Arabs had no control. Fears and suspicions of Western domination, which were historically justified, gained ground rapidly. The sins of Saddam, who was the first to blame for provoking this hurricane, were easily overlooked.

Indeed, the failure of the West to show the same strength of feeling over Palestine as it did over Kuwait was another factor which influenced the views of many Arabs and Moslems — Palestinians in particular. It was widely asked why the Americans had never contemplated similar action to counter 23 years of occupation of Arab land by Israel. The Americans seemed to consider that persuasion was enough as far as the Israelis were concerned but not sufficient to solve internal Arab problems. For those Arabs, the duplicity and hypocrisy of the West was so blatant that claims of morality in 'liberating Kuwait' by the US-led forces were seen as a mockery. The views of the majority of Arabs were more a sign of defiance of the West than complacency over Kuwait or support for Saddam.

Misreading the support he enjoyed from the West while fighting against Iran, Saddam thought that he would be allowed to expand his regional power without confrontation with the United States. Since 1988 when the war with Iran ended, Saddam had indulged in a rope-pulling game with the Americans who were determined to limit his power.

Saddam decided to invade Kuwait for his own reasons, which were mainly financial. Convinced that there would be no war, he then brought God, Palestine, the Pan-Arab cause and the redistribution of wealth into the picture. It was an ideal banner with which to exploit, fully and crudely, genuine and widespread resentment against the legacy of a colonial system which is still in force in much of the Arab world. The political immaturity of undemocratic systems encouraged a spontaneous outburst of feeling in an unequal confrontation. But in the final analysis Saddam — who decided alone to invade Kuwait — dragged the Arabs, or most of them, with him to a tragic and humiliating defeat. This was the second time in recent history, after their defeat in the 1967 war with Israel, that the Arabs had to come to this sad and bitter end. On both occasions they were trapped or led into a confrontation they had never sought and which was gravely mishandled by their self-appointed leaders.

Costs and dilemmas

The Palestinians seem doomed to suffer most from this crisis. At a human level those in the diaspora will be the first victims of a tribal nationalism which is sweeping the Arab world. They are the displaced, unwanted minorities which Arab governments have feared most while paying lip service to their cause. They will be subjected to more discrimination in terms of education, work and freedom of movement, and will be denied any political freedom. Thousands will suffer the effects of economic devastation as they are forced to leave Kuwait and the other Gulf states which they helped to build over decades. Many have nowhere to go.

As for those still living under Israeli occupation, many will lose the income they received from relatives in the Gulf. They have no opportunity for economic development as their land and water have been taken. They have been permitted to serve the Israeli economy as virtual slave labour — and are now facing increasing competition from Soviet Jewish immigrants. The curfew imposed by the Israeli military during the Gulf crisis in the West Bank and Gaza administered a further blow to the livelihood of the Palestinians.

At the political level, the PLO has been the victim of a deliberate campaign to create misunderstanding. Its efforts to avoid military confrontation were ignored by the US administration and its Arab friends. Ill-advised statements, designed mainly for domestic consumption, were made by some Palestinian leaders during the crisis and were picked up by the Western media which interpreted them as supporting Saddam's actions in Kuwait. The Israelis and the Americans were quick to claim that the Palestinian leadership had lost all political and international credibility, concluding that the PLO could not be considered an acceptable partner in any peace negotiations. Yet this had been the view of the Israelis and the Americans all along, well before the Gulf crisis! They are the only countries, together with South Africa, who do not recognise the Palestinians' right to self-determination and the PLO as their legitimate representative. New excuses had to be invented for old policies.

The Palestinians' dilemma is that their right to statehood and freedom from oppression and occupation apparently depend on their good behaviour. If they are found 'supporting Saddam' then their rights can be called into question by the Americans who are nevertheless prepared to deal with brutal and undemocratic regimes when it suits them. How can one describe the Israeli behaviour, then, — its refusal to comply with the international will, its daily violation of human rights in the occupied territories, its co-operation with the apartheid regime in South Africa and its arms supplies to the most ruthless dictatorships in Latin America?

The real issue is this: where do the two sides — Palestinians and Israelis — each stand on the peace principles which are universally accepted? In November 1988 the Palestinian National Council endorsed the peace initiative, which still stands. In December of the same year, at a special session in Geneva of the United Nations General Assembly, Arafat told the world that a two-state solution based on 1967 borders is the Palestinian goal, that the Palestinians accepted UN Resolution 242 and recognised Israel's right to exist. Arafat reiterated this position during the Gulf crisis and resumed his peace offensive after the war, offering PLO acceptance of a UN buffer zone on the borders with Israel, Jewish citizens of the state of Palestine and Jewish cabinet members. He showed flexibility on territory if the Israelis agreed to do the same. The PLO has dismissed all along any suggestions that the *intifada* should abandon civil disobedience for armed violence, stating clearly that dialogue with the Israeli peace groups should continue.

In contrast the official Israeli position has become increasingly intransigent over the last decade. It has not yet accepted the principle of withdrawal to 1967 borders as required by UN Resolutions 242 and 338. It has formally annexed East Jerusalem and the Syrian Golan Heights and still occupies a large area of southern Lebanon, refusing to implement Resolution 425. Israel still adamantly refuses to talk to the PLO, bans any contacts with the organisation and refuses to recognise the Palestinians' right to self-determination. Israel is pursuing its harsh policies unchallenged in the occupied territories, annexing Arab land, building new settlements, subjecting the Arabs to torture, imprisonment, deportations, almost daily killings, collective punishment, starvation and economic destruction. While the world was preoccupied with the Gulf crisis, Shamir clung to his hard line position, erecting barriers to any future settlement.

The PLO is the only available framework for the Palestinian people in their struggle for nationhood and symbolises their aspiration to live in their own free and independent state. It includes representatives from all political groups and communities in Palestine and the diaspora, bringing together trade unionists and independent activists and religious and public figures. The PLO and the demand for Palestinians' rights are clearly inseparable. As the British journalist David Hirst has pointed out: 'If Americans, Europeans, Arabs and Israelis now conspire to say "bye bye to Arafat", they will for the foreseeable future be saying "bye bye" to the Palestinians rights.'

The only positive result of the Gulf crisis for the Palestinians has been the proposal to link Iraqi withdrawal from Kuwait with Israeli withdrawal from the occupied territories which had the merit of drawing the attention of the Arabs and the world community to the other pending unresolved crisis. The Americans, who dismissed the proposal before the war as unworthy of serious consideration, now find it difficult to overlook. Given the role of global leadership assumed by the United States during the Gulf crisis Washington felt obliged, in order to sustain its position and credibility, to include the resolution of the Arab-Israeli conflict on the post-war agenda. Indeed, the resolution of the Palestinian question remains the key to any settlement aimed at achieving peace, arms control, stability and development in the region.

But Israeli intransigence and the blank-cheque support it still enjoys from the United States remain the main obstacles to any peaceful settlement. Previous experience has proved that peace in the Middle East needs a radical change of attitude and fresh thinking from the American side. If the Americans seek to enforce their own order based on old doctrines, it will only lead to further turbulence in the Middle East.

So far the Americans have not gone beyond cautious and vague formulations and have shown disturbing signs of intending to apply old and unworkable remedies. Confronted with stubbornness and blackmail from the Israeli side, and fears and submission from the Arab side, the US administration seems more willing to pressure the Arab states for further concessions, sustaining the old view that Israel will come to its senses by persuasion rather than pressure. Financial aid was pumped to Israel during the Gulf crisis over and above its annual subsidy of US$3.5 billion. The United States also assured Israel that it could keep its arsenal of nuclear, chemical and other weapons of mass destruction, while proposing that the Arab side should be stripped of the right to possess or produce such weapons in the future.

The Americans seem trapped with their old policies towards the Palestinians: no to the PLO, no to the Palestinian state, while still entertaining schemes which fall short of full implementation of the Palestinian right of self-determination. US efforts focus on ending the state of war between Arab states and Israel while addressing the Palestinian question only in a nominal way. The Americans are pushing for a twin-track approach with parallel Arab-Israeli and Palestinian-Israeli negotiations. Direct and separate Arab-Israeli negotiations will be carried out within a regional conference formula under their auspices with a ceremonial role or no role at all for the UN, the Europeans or the Soviet Union — in short, a revamped Camp David process.

If a regional conference is held, it will be presented by the United States as a step forward. But it will be seen as a very divisive measure in the Arab world — as the negation of previous agreements that the only way forward is a genuinely international conference. Even if the United States succeeds in promoting a Camp David-style solution between Israel and Jordan, it will not address the fundamental problems. Firstly, it will further undermine the position of its Arab allies by exposing their subservience to US foreign policy. Secondly, it will not even begin to tackle the human and political dimensions of the Palestinian question, as the United States would find it very difficult to find an alternative to the PLO in any talks. The Palestinians are not going to surrender their only real achievement gained over the past 25 years — the right to speak for themselves and not through the voice of an Arab government.

With its military success in the Gulf, the United States now seems tempted by the solution outlined by James Baker well before the Gulf crisis: Jordan is the Palestinian state, the occupied territories are to be ruled in accordance with the basic guidelines of the Israeli government with only limited Palestinian autonomy, and the political representatives of the Palestinians will be chosen for them. While the PLO will be excluded, and the Palestinian leadership either imprisoned or deported, new Israeli excuses will be hailed as generous steps forward. Peace in the Middle East therefore looks as remote as ever. One track of the twin-track approach — the Palestinian-Israeli negotiation — will be blocked, while the other — the Arab-Israeli negotiation — will end up achieving very little.

Syria and Egypt and the spoils of war

Youssef Choueiri

Syria and Egypt joined the allied coalition out of self-interest. Youssef Choueiri describes how they have received their reward

We should not underestimate the United States as a world power, ridicule its policies or accuse the Americans of being unable to understand history. After all, it is they who are making it nowadays. One of the ironies of this war is that the victors have actually ended up purporting to adopt the demands put forward by the vanquished: Palestine, economic development, an equitable distribution of wealth and security. It is even more ironic that the original aims of this war, often obscured by lofty ideals, were once again reaffirmed: access to oil supplies and their protection. The motives of Arab participants in the war, such as Syria and Egypt, also need to be examined coolly and in terms of their real interests.

Democracy, however, is conspicuous by its absence from the programmes of the Arab and US leaderships. In a sense, one could say that Saudi Arabia has emerged as the main victor, having seen Iraq's war machine smashed to pieces. Democracy remains an undesirable innovation that both Americans and the Saudis do not wish to impose either on others or on themselves.

Syria is another country that stands to benefit from the spoils of a victorious war. It has already hosted a meeting of the Gulf states and Egypt and on 6 March the foreign ministers of Syria, Egypt and the six-member Gulf Co-operation Council announced in Damascus the formation of a broad pact to ensure Gulf security and economic development. This pact envisaged turning the Syrian and Egyptian forces now in the Gulf into the core of an Arab peace-keeping force to protect the region against threats of subversion or invasion. This force was further depicted as being the foundation stone of a wider Arab system of defence. Other Arab states were called upon to join. The eight foreign ministers also stressed their support for the Arab League, its charter and role as the foremost institution of Arab solidarity.

While the excluded Arab states remained sceptical, Israel announced its willingness to co-ordinate its policies with the eight members of the coalition and join them at least as an associate member. But Iran objected to such security arrangements and even ridiculed the idea of having Syrian forces to protect the sovereignty of Gulf states while the same forces 'have failed over many years to recover the Israeli-occupied Golan heights'. The United States and its allies in Europe, however, welcomed the idea as a positive development. The following day, President George Bush told a joint session of Congress that the time had come to put an end to the Arab-Israeli conflict and accept the principle of exchanging land for peace.

But why did Syria and Egypt join this war in the first place? And what do they stand to gain from it? First, both countries have fought and lost successive wars against Israel ever since its foundation in 1948. Joining a losing party once again was not an option they could afford to entertain. Second, the two countries were the leaders of Pan-Arabism and socialism throughout the 1950s and 1960s. It was only after 1973 and the meteoric rise in oil prices that they began to lose their central role in the Arab world. Aware of their limited clout, they chose to defend the status quo.

Third, Egypt had already signed a peaceful treaty with Israel, forsaking the option of war to solve the Arab-Israeli dispute, and had aligned itself with the United States in its foreign policy. The co-operation of Egypt and Iraq during the Iran-Iraq war stemmed from the same consideration. Syria, on the other hand, persisted in its refusal to sign a similar treaty with Israel as the latter had annexed the Golan Heights and was in no mood for compromise. Syria's idea of achieving strategic parity with Israel, however, received a severe blow in its confrontation in 1982. A few years later President Gorbachev informed President Assad of Moscow's reluctance to offer unconditional assistance and advised him to seek a diplomatic solution to his relations with Israel. Abandoned by the Soviet Union, Assad embarked on various attempts to rehabilitate Syria and break its diplomatic isolation.

Fourth, the economies of both countries were witnessing steadily falling productivity, mounting foreign debt and diminishing hard currency. The Gulf crisis afforded an opportunity to write off debts, gain access to fresh funds, and impose or improve their balance of trade. While Egypt had at least US$13 billion owed to US and Gulf creditors written off, Syria has so far received about US$2 billion in direct aid from Gulf countries. Open-door policies in both countries introduced after 1973 were also an incentive to align themselves with the states that had at their disposal advanced technologies, capital and aid programmes.

Fifth, Syria saw the Gulf crisis as a golden opportunity to liquidate the remnants of Maronite resistance to its influence in Lebanon. The surrender of General Michel Aoun, who was thought to be backed by the Iraqi President, and the reluctance of the United States and Israel to intervene, brought most of Lebanon under Syria's control.

It is also important to take into account the fierce rivalry between Damascus and Baghdad for political, military and ideological influence in the Fertile Crescent. While Damascus extends various kinds of assistance to various Iraqi opposition groups, Baghdad acts as a host to the main opponents of the Syrian regime — the Moslem Brotherhood. Ever since the Iran-Iraq war, this rivalry has intensified and King Hussein of Jordan has failed on many occasions to heal the rift between the two leaders. Last but not least, both states possess the efficient means to contain unrest or widespread civil disturbances. In fact, a state of emergency exists in both states.

Syria, having restored its central role in the Arab-Israeli conflict, is now being courted by the United States and the Soviet Union as well as the Gulf states. Israel's approach to Syria is more complicated. On the one hand, it offers direct talks leading to a bilateral agreement and, on the other, insists on pointing at Assad's endeavours to replenish his arsenal of weapons in preparation for armed conflict. Syria's long-established links with Iran places it in a unique position to act as a broker between Tehran and its gulf neighbours. Jordan is another country that is expected to co-ordinate its future policies with Syria or at least seek Syria's good offices to bring it back into the fold of Gulf creditors.

As to the long-term effects of the war, it would appear that the euphoria that greeted the collapse of the Soviet Union, as well as the military victory in the Gulf, has been rapidly eroded. The world may well turn out, after all, to consist of the same power blocs with competing strategies and divergent interests. The cause of democracy in the Arab world has been dealt a severe blow. Security and oil are the long-term objectives of the West. Certain Arab countries are to be rewarded by allowing them a share in policing the Gulf. They would also be offered the opportunity to sell their cheap labour to a number of reconstruction firms and other companies. But what is the immediate function of an armed Arab peace-keeping force in the Gulf? It may turn out to be a tool for the repression of internal popular unrest rather than the repulsion of invasion. After all, Iraq and its army are supposed to be in ruins. The plight of the Kurds adds another illustration of the futility of military might in solving the human problems of a troubled Middle East.

4
A BLIGHTED FUTURE

An experiment in the unknown

Fred Pearce

As scientists discovered, the Gulf War has had gruesome environmental effects. The full extent of the damage, Fred Pearce writes, is still impossible to predict

At 10am on 21 February 1991, Iraqi troops unwittingly launched one of the most unnerving scientific experiments ever. They began setting fire to large numbers of Kuwaiti oil wells, unleashing on the planet one of the largest palls of smoke seen in recent centuries. The smoke was first revealed to independent observers on images taken by Europe's Meteosat weather satellite. Scientists at Imperial College, London, saw the first smoke emerge from close to the Burgan oilfield in central Kuwait that morning. By 4pm, the satellite showed smoke billowing from the Sabriya field to the north and, by 7pm, yet more was coming from the nearby Rar Rawdatyan field. Kuwait was ablaze.

In these final hours before Iraq's first acceptance of a Soviet ceasefire plan, more than 500 well-heads, many long since abandoned by oil companies, were set ablaze by the detonation of explosives laid months before. It was more than a month before the first fire was extinguished on 7 April and fire fighters brought to the scene warned that it could be more than a year before the fires were put out and the great black clouds engulfing Kuwait would disappear. Within days of the firing of the wells, a dense plume of black smoke had stretched for 600 kilometres down the Gulf, past Bahrain and towards the Straits of Hormuz, where the smoke finally dispersed on the winds and spread as an almost invisible haze across the Indian Ocean. For a day the smoke blew back across Iraq. And on 27 February, when winds dropped to dead calm, it formed a black pall that covered the whole of Kuwait as the allied ground troops retook the country.

Shadow of damage
Since that first week, the pattern has persisted, with smoke being

continuously belched from the Kuwaiti fields, and blowing generally south and east before dispersing into the tropical atmosphere. Over Kuwait, the dense black smoke created a 'darkness at noon', when temperatures were as much as ten degrees Celsius below normal. Scientists warned that the particles of soot created as the oil burned had unique optical properties. A single gram of soot could blot out almost all sunlight over an area of around ten square metres. A month's soot had the potential to cover an area half the size of the United States.

Luckily this has not happened in practice. This is because the smoke has not reached as high into the atmosphere as some atmospheric modellers predicted during January before the fires began. It has reached two to five rather than the predicted ten to 15 kilometres. The apparent reason was that, however fierce the fires appeared on television screens, the heat from the burning was not sufficient to create the thermal currents that could have taken the smoke into the upper atmosphere. The only smoke that reached such heights came from the short-lived but more intense conflagrations that occurred when Iraqi saboteurs and allied forces bombed oil installations in Kuwait and southern Iraq.

The low height reached by the smoke turned out, in the first weeks at least, to be bad news for Kuwait but good news for the rest of Asia. The low trajectory of the smoke as it streamed away from the oil fields meant that much of it was incorporated into clouds, falling to the ground within a few hours or days as sticky, black and probably very acid rain. The rest, blowing down the Gulf, remained within the range of surface winds that either brought it to the ground or dispersed it. Dispersion happened much more swiftly than if the smoke had reached the rarefied air above the weather systems. The average residence time of the smoke in the atmosphere can be measured in weeks, rather than the months or years if it had reached higher.

For this reason, predictions that a large cloud of smoke could shade the sun over large areas of the Middle East and southern Asia, which had been made by a committee of eminent atmospheric scientists meeting in the United States in mid-January, were not fulfilled. Instead the smoke fell out over Kuwait and its neighbours. But in other respects the dire warnings of those accused at the time of alarmism did come true. Their initial estimates that between 1.5 and 3 million barrels of oil a day would burn appeared to be about correct, though the Kuwaiti authorities suggested that the true figure could be 5 million tonnes or more. And if anything, the 'alarmists' had been over-optimistic in predicting that it might take a year to put out the fires.

Reports soon emerged of the immediate effects of the fallout of this smoke. Kuwaiti doctors reported that many young, elderly and frail citizens were suffering from lung complaints. (Health officials, anxious not to put off visitors, denied the stories.) The nearest available comparison appeared to be with the 'pea-souper' smogs that once afflicted Britain for a few days every year or so. But while these smogs lasted perhaps a week and sometimes killed many hundreds, the Kuwaiti smog continued on and off for many weeks. Many of the contaminants created when oil burns in the open air, such as benzene compounds, are thought to be carcinogenic. But cancers take a long time to develop and it could be many years before doctors can assess whether cancer rates increase — another deadly scientific experiment in the making.

Among the Gulf states, the smoke has been causing black, oily and acid rain. Flights over the Gulf by a research plane owned by the Meteorological Office in Britain confirmed the presence of large amounts of sulphur, which converts in clouds to sulphuric acid. This acid fallout may damage crops in southern Iraq and Iran, and black rain was reported as far away as Turkey. The clouds could also reduce the amount of sunlight falling on some crops, leading to smaller yields.

One little-considered effect of the large amounts of soot is that it could increase rainfall over the Gulf by 'seeding' clouds, that is, providing nuclei around which tiny droplets of moisture can coalesce into larger raindrops that fall from the cloud as rain. The local rainy season lasts through the spring to April, and during March there were many reports of unusually heavy flooding in southern Iran, which cut off hundreds of villages. Iran was in the path of much of the soot from Kuwait, but it is impossible to do more than conjecture whether the two events are linked.

The worst possible consequence of the fires, made in predictions in January, was that the smoke could disrupt the Asian monsoons during the summer. The reasoning was that a pall of black smoke, once established in the upper atmosphere, would take a year or more to be washed out in the rains. Meanwhile, by reducing the sunlight over parts of Asia, it could prevent the land warming up as the summer progressed. This might dampen down the monsoon winds, which are essentially a giant sea breeze created when the land becomes warmer than the sea, hot air rises and moist ocean is sucked in beneath it. Computer simulations of what might happen to the climate after a global nuclear exchange set off widespread fires across the planet had produced this effect with a similar amount of smoke over the tropics to that being produced from the Kuwaiti fires burning today. The failure of the smoke to penetrate the upper atmosphere now makes such an extreme event much less likely. But with so much smoke accumulating in the atmosphere over the tropics, few climate modellers were inclined to rule out the possibility. And as reports in early April indicated that black snow was falling over the Himalayas, it was clear that, even though the black clouds were breaking up before they left the Gulf, the smoke was spreading slowly round the planet.

Warnings ignored

Official responses among the allies to the early warnings of environmental catastrophes from the Gulf War were revealing. When environmentalists in Britain and the United States first raised the issue in early January, their fears were dismissed by ministers. At the British Department of Energy, John Wakeham emitted a barrage of claims that 'recent reports' were 'misleading', though a detailed reading of his statement showed that he was referring only to a possible 'greenhouse effect' from carbon dioxide created by burning oil. (This was a red herring since the oil was only expected to burn at the rate at which, in peacetime, it would have been pumped from the ground and burned round the world in power stations and car engines. Apart from King Hussein of Jordan, nobody had predicted that the planet would fry — rather the reverse).

Departmental officials leaked to British Labour member of parliament Tam Dalyell their misgivings that the data supplied to Wakeham by his scientists had been misused. The truth of these allegations became clearer when the Meteorological Office published its own detailed assessment of the 'worst case scenario', which agreed in almost every particular with the claims of John Cox, an industrial chemist whose warnings at a meeting organised by members of the Campaign for Nuclear Disarmament began the debate. Likewise officials on both sides of the Atlantic gave scant credence to the claims of an American consultant to the oil industry, Richard Golob, who predicted with startling accuracy how the Iraqis could sabotage oil installations in the Gulf to create a giant oil slick. Only after the fires were lit and the oil slicks unleashed did the allied governments abandon their disdain and cry loudly that Iraq was unleashing 'environmental terrorism' on the world. At this stage, the scale of the actions was exaggerated, first by the Saudis who overestimated the size of the oil leak, and then by the Kuwaitis who hyped the size of the smoke clouds.

One reason for wailing so loudly about the oil slick was that much of it (possibly most of it) came not from Iraq opening the taps on an oil pipeline but from oil tankers at anchor in the Gulf that had been bombed by allied forces. The ITN pictures which first showed birds dying as an oil slick hit the Saudi coast were almost certainly not the result of Iraqi eco-terrorism.

The initial response of the Saudi authorities to the oil slick was to call on the international community to help it protect the environment, while in practice devoting all the oil booms and skimmers that swiftly reached its shores to protect industrial plant and desalinisation works. This was understandable, especially given Saudi Arabia's reliance on desalinisation for its water supplies. But it struck a sour note with environmentalists whose offer of help to identify and protect wildlife refuges, such as islands where turtles were due to lay their eggs, coral reefs, and submerged areas of sea grasses where fish breed and dugongs live, were spurned.

As the oil slick became becalmed off the Saudi coast, international interest in the slick dimmed. It came as a surprise in early April to learn that the slick was still being fed by leaks from oil installations that nobody had found time to plug. Oil industry experts calculated that, despite Saudi exaggerations of the size of the slick, it remained some 20 times larger than the Exxon Valdez spill in Alaska two years before. Because of the sluggish nature of sea currents in the Gulf, ocean modellers warned that it could be washing round the Gulf for a year or more before finding its way into the Indian Ocean. It would, ecologists said, probably be decades before the Gulf fully recovered.

There are undoubtedly many environmental surprises still to be provided by the aftermath of the Gulf War. In April it was still unclear what damage allied bombing of bridges across the rivers Tigris and Euphrates had done to the complex system of dams and barrages, many of which double as bridges and which are vital to the ancient system of river management that maintains irrigation for Iraqi crops and prevents widespread flooding. Since the first Mesopotamian cities were formed here thousands of years ago, life in this near-desert landscape has been so dependent on engineering works to control these waters that the phrase 'hydraulic civilisations' was coined to describe the early empires. If the barrages were breached, as seemed likely, water from the late spring snowmelt in Turkey could not be diverted into canals that water fields of cotton and cereals. And near the mouth of the two rivers, any breached dykes would be certain to flood huge areas of low-lying land in the marshy south of the country.

Contamination of water supplies is another major concern. In the weeks after hostilities ended, fears grew of epidemics of cholera and typhoid in southern Iraq, where the destruction of water and sewage works and loss of electricity supplies to pump clean water, led to millions of people drinking polluted water from the rivers. But there could be equally serious longer-term problems, not least in Saudi Arabia. The hundreds of thousands of allied forces in the north of that country for many months created massive amounts of waste oil and sewage, much of which was poured directly into the sand. This was done in a region where underground water reservoirs are critical both for drinking water and to irrigate crops. These underground stores of water were laid down in wetter times and are not replenished. If they have been contaminated, then they will have been lost for good.

Polluted sands

The desert sands themselves have been widely assumed to be a wasteland invulnerable to environmental damage. There is, the argument goes, nothing there worth saving. This leaves aside the permanent damage probably done to the lives of the Bedouin — the only people in the region with no interest in the borders over which more 'advanced' communities around them fought. Wartime pictures of tanks driving past camels were poignant. In the aftermath of war, Bedouins and their camels face trekking through a desert peppered with unexploded mines and the debris of war.

But what of the sand itself? One little-considered consequence of the presence of the allied forces in the desert could be an increase in dust storms that could last for decades. An Egyptian-born geologist, Farouk El-Baz, warned in the American journal *Science* in March that a stabilising 'crust' on the surface of the desert sands that had taken hundreds of years to form had been destroyed within a few weeks by tanks and other heavy vehicles. As the desert evolved over the past 3,000 years, the wind has blown away many fine sand grains, leaving a hard surface layer of small pebbles, which El-Baz dubs a 'desert shield'. Allied carpet bombing, tanks and the digging of trenches by the Iraqis has destroyed much of this shield, leaving the sands beneath open to the winds. He predicted 'a new generation of sand dunes marching southward' through Kuwait along the coast of the Gulf for hundreds of miles as far as Qatar and the United Arab Emirates. 'The war has done tremendous damage to the surface of the land', he wrote. 'The consequences will be felt in the region for decades.'

This is one more unknown in a long line of gruesome experiments on the environment that the war has provided for scientists. One final such experiment relates to the soot falling over the Himalayas. Two years ago, the Indian government got into trouble with environmentalists for proposing a series of experiments aimed at speeding up the melting of snow in these mountains to increase the flow in mighty rivers such as the Ganges during periods of low flow in April and May. The Central Water Commission in New Delhi proposed speeding up the spring thaw by spraying coal dust onto the snowpack. The dust would absorb the sun's heat and induce thawing of the snow. Now it seems that the Gulf War may have carried out the experiment for them, but on a far bigger scale than their scientists dreamed.

The post-war Arab world: Development in reverse

Rami Zreik

Arab co-operation for development has been severely set back by the Gulf War. In spite of oil wealth, the region will depend more heavily on the North. Rami Zreik argues that the New World Order is hostile to development of the South

The Arab world is slowly awakening to the consequences of one of the major disasters in its modern history: the war against Iraq. There can be little doubt that the damage caused by the Gulf conflict will go beyond the physical effect of bombing Iraq back into the 19th century. As many anti-war analysts predicted, evidence so far suggests the cost of the war will be heavy on the whole region and will probably affect other countries in the South. A look at the Arab world today shows that the various processes of political and economic change, especially those linked to the much sought-after Arab unity, are now at their lowest ebb since the concept of Arabism was created.

Many would argue that the modern Arab world has always been plagued by political discord. The causes, it is agreed, lie in a combination of blatant interventionism by the industrialised North and Israel and a long procession of ruthless totalitarian regimes. The regression witnessed in the aftermath of this divisive conflict would therefore seem to be the continuation of a natural process.

Yet this war may have taken the division a dangerous step further, creating inter-Arab schisms of unprecedented proportions. These are certain to affect the Arab world on many levels, altering, for instance, the course of the nascent efforts for concerted regional development. Joint endeavour for development has been on the Arab agenda for many decades now. This concept has taken different forms over the years, ranging from total Arab unity during Nasser's days to the more recent pragmatic approaches based on mutual economic, cultural or educational interest such as the Gulf Co-operation Council and the Arab Co-operation Council. In spite of their ideological differences, these initiatives have in common the desire to promote the development of the Arab nation as a self-ruling entity, in control of its own resources and providing sustainable services and welfare to its citizens. In the wake of the war, the prospect of the Arab world becoming a viable economic entity looks at best, imperilled. The concept of global Arab development is in danger of becoming obsolete, and the Arab countries are in danger of returning to a state of colonial protection, under the custody of the mighty North.

Development priorities

Development has many aspects and the relative importance of each depends on the status of the country. In the poorest countries, a priority is the provision of the most basic services such as water, health and education. The middle-income countries usually enjoy a higher level of basic services and therefore have a different approach. Thus, alongside the upkeep and improvement of basic services, economic self-reliance is given a high priority with industry, trade, and agriculture targeted for improvement and expansion. Many Arab countries, especially in the Middle East, fall into the middle-income bracket, but, like most countries in the South, are still plagued by technological dependence on the North. The historical reason is simple: the sudden imposition of the colonising technologically advanced West on the less advanced colonised regions caused the destruction of almost all existing indigenous systems.

Thus, in today's South, nearly all basic services, agriculture, domestic needs and the embryonic industries are extremely reliant on imported goods and technologies. The Arab Gulf states, for instance, produce oil in quantities, but have little means of converting this into petrochemical by-products. The Fertile Crescent countries rely both on imported technologies for food production and on subsidised imports to feed their populations. The water-scarce Arab countries depend on imported desalinisation technologies for their survival. To develop, these countries now need to catch up on the various technologies involved, not by importing them, but by understanding how they work and adapting them to local requirements. In the process, it is essential that a body of scientists and researchers should emerge. Sustainable development in these states thus requires progress in the fields of science and technology. Unfortunately no Arab country can afford the costs of such a process.

In the pre-Gulf War Arab Middle East, a strategy for scientific advancement and securing the transfer of appropriate technology had not yet been put into action. But there were clear signs that many countries were on the right track. In recent years, Kuwait, Saudi Arabia and Jordan had witnessed an explosion in scientific research, doubling their output of scientific publications every three to four years (against a world average of eight to ten years). In this area, they had already surpassed major countries in the South such as Turkey, Iran and Pakistan. Iraq, although more interested in gearing its science to military technology, was also doing well. The war, however, has destroyed Kuwaiti and Iraqi technological capability, and severely crippled the Saudis and the Jordanians, thus damaging the prospects for development. But the damage caused by the war will go well beyond the physical destruction of scientific and technological facilities. Indeed, its effect on political and economic developments in the region may be much more long-term. Major changes are already occurring.

From co-operation to disintegration

Development, especially in the field of science and technology, requires a framework in which it can occur. Three components are essential: wealth (and control over it), expertise and political stability. Most Southern countries are not fortunate enough to have access to more than one, relying on aid and goodwill from the wealthier North in order to develop. In a few countries, however, not all development is dependant on foreign aid. The Arab World, if taken as a single entity, with the wealth of oil, expertise and huge labour resources, would seem set for success. But this would require a fourth ingredient — Arab co-operation.

Co-operation among the Arab countries is paradoxically the weakest link in the chain that joins them. Yet through organisations like the Arab League or other efforts at unity like the Gulf Co-operation Council a rosier future was slowly unfolding. The Gulf War has severely set back Arab co-operation, jeopardised the exchange of expertise and control over wealth and increased regional instability. With its four main components critically undermined, the essential framework for development is slowly collapsing.

One of the most striking aspects of the war, and one that the North used to give itself credibility, was the conflict between Arab countries over the war. The Arab people, like many peoples in the South, gave almost unanimous support to Saddam Hussein, in spite of strong reservations about his character or system of government. Yet some Arab rulers, through fear or through need, chose to support the United States in its destruction of Iraq. This led to a severe deepening of existing schisms and to the semi-disintegration of the region. An accurate reflection of the situation has been provided by the Arab League, which split in August 1990 over US participation in the war. This has so far caused the League to move its headquarters to Egypt from the more neutral Tunis and to have difficulties in electing a secretary-general. The expected collapse of the League's various commissions dealing with agriculture, science, education and technology are a clear sign that Arab co-operation for development is moving backwards. Another sign of the times is the increased difficulty faced by Arab nationals when travelling between Arab states. It is, for instance, now harder for a Jordanian to be granted entrance into Egypt than it is for an Israeli, even though both Jordan and Egypt are members of the Arab Co-operation Council. Palestinians, Jordanians, Yemenis and, to a certain extent Lebanese, are now, as a group, *personae non grata* in the Gulf countries. This is bound to have a major effect on the exchange of expertise within the Arab world.

Such an atmosphere of xenophobic suspicion can already be felt in the field of scientific and technological exchanges. Scientific research in the Arab world had recently started to involve groups of Arab scientists drawn from various countries of origin. Many worked under one umbrella, usually in institutes in the Gulf region, where funds are available. Before the war, much of the research in the Gulf was carried out by Arab scientists and technicians from the poorer Middle East, such as Palestinians, Lebanese and Jordanians. In the period before the war, however, many Gulf states embarked on a nationalisation movement, replacing foreign Arabs with nationals, regardless of their qualifications or skills. The new splits in the region have exacerbated this trend, and it has become increasingly difficult for many people of the above nationalities to live in the Gulf states. Tens of thousands of Palestinians and Jordanians have so far left the Gulf, leaving behind a significant skills gap. This was well-illustrated by the unreasonably long time it took Kuwait to restore essential services after Iraqi withdrawal. This situation is worsening now as more people are under pressure to leave, they are returning to countries with crippled economies where gaining employment is increasingly difficult. In turn, this has led to a serious emigration problem and to the much-dreaded brain drain to the North.

This loss of expertise, skills and knowledge is certain to take its toll on the development of the whole Arab world. The most hard-hit countries will naturally be Iraq and Kuwait and, in the longer term, Jordan and Saudi Arabia. Little news has so far trickled from Iraq, but the situation in Kuwait is starting to come to light. Of the the 1,000 plus staff members of the Kuwait Institute for Scientific Research (KISR), only 10-15 per cent now remain. Adnan Shihab-Eldin, a senior researcher at KISR, believes that no more than half of the staff will return. Similar bodies relying on non-Kuwaiti Arab expertise will inevitably be affected. This post-war loosening of the natural links within the Arab world is to a large extent sponsored by the rich Gulf states. These states, paradoxically the greatest winners and losers in the war, are naively attempting to protect their wealth from other Arabs. Indeed, the poorer Arab countries not fortunate enough to have had their post-colonial borders drawn enclosing oil fields have always argued for their right to a fair share of this wealth to improve their lot. After this war, they will have less space in which to make such demands.

Arab oil wealth, the centre pivot of development plans, has been hard hit by the war. One of the North's reasons for the war was to strengthen its grip over one-quarter of the world's oil production. The North wished to avoid oil falling into Arab hands it might not always be able to control, and being used for purposes it did not approve of. The fact is that Arab capital never really belonged to the Arabs. Indeed, most of the oil money has always gone towards strengthening the North's economy — recycled into Northern banks, spent on foreign imports or invested overseas. Moreover, although the Gulf countries are net aid donors (US$2.4 billions in 1988, mostly to Muslim and other Arab countries), their contribution was never significant enough to trigger real change. Arab aid had decreased well before the war, having fallen from US$9.54 billion in 1980. In the wake of the war, the financing of development in poor Arab countries by the rich ones, and thus the financing of pan-Arab developmental co-operation, has been compromised.

The rich countries, especially Saudi Arabia and Kuwait, might not even be able to afford the cost of development anymore given the size of their bill at the end of the war. They must honour their pledge to pay 80 per cent of the war's cost (amounting to nearly US$40 billion) and pay for the reconstruction of Kuwait (estimated at US$50 billion), as well as eventually, for that of Iraq. A bill with a twist, as only the United States is likely to benefit financially.

The expected costs for the Gulf states do not stop here: swept away by the war technophilia, Arab states are now under pressure to purchase the weapons they have seen in action. Recent reports have indicated that the United States is planning to sell the Arab states and Turkey US$18 billion worth of arms. With Saudi Arabia and Kuwait already obliged to borrow abroad, it is unclear whether any of the Gulf states will have enough money to cover the costs, as a significant increase in oil production seems unlikely. The war will thus have emptied the money baskets of the Arab world, destroying for many countries the dreams of development independent of Northern aid.

These changes are not of the sort that breed political stability. Prior to the Gulf War, and in the wake of the events in Eastern Europe, many Arab rulers had started to bow to the pressures for democratisation. In the post-war context, internal dissent is becoming more acute as many opposition movements protest against the governments who have abandoned Iraq. Many regimes are now expected to revert to or continue to rule by repression, but this time with the blessing of the United States and its allies. We have probably only seen a taste of what is still to come. During the Gulf War, Egypt, Morocco and Syria severely repressed the tens of thousands who took to the streets to protest against their governments' support for the war. Kuwait is in political havoc, with internal strife between the opposition, the resistance and the Sabbah regime compounded by the daily oppression of Palestinians and other Arabs. Iraq is shattered by insurrection in the north and the south, quelled at high human and material cost. A just solution to the Palestinian problem seems further away than ever. Such a situation is not propitious for the flourishing of freedom and democracy, which is crucial to the achievement of genuine progress. Many of the educated Arab elite might choose to leave the region for calmer havens. This brain drain is certain to affect most sectors, but it will have an especially debilitating impact on higher education. A similar process occurred during the war in Lebanon, and has resulted in schools and universities producing incompletely educated graduates.

A grim taste of the New World Order

The future looks gloomy for development in the Arab countries, individually and collectively. The war appears to have severely set back the developmental process. The prerequisites for a concerted Arab developmental effort seem further away than ever. The path to development, once opened by oil, has been closed, perhaps for decades to come. A new protectionist system is in the process of being finalised; a system in which the North will maintain decaying regimes for the sake of protecting its interests in the region. Those countries who can afford technology will have to buy it and forget once and for all about its transfer and adaptation to local needs.

But this new order has further implications. In the South, local development of resources in nearly every field relies heavily on the North as a source of research and up-to-date knowledge. Iraq's progress in civil and military technology was largely due to its ability to tap these sources. Thus, Western fears that another Arab country might one day follow Iraq's example and step outside its limits is understandable. Access to Northern scientific knowledge will probably be limited to the minimum by an intellectual embargo not unlike that imposed on Iraq in the years preceding the crisis. Increased instability in the Arab world is bound to make any high-tech foreign company think twice before investing, thus depriving Arabs of another potential source of knowledge.

Within the Arab World, the split between rich and poor countries is reaching levels never attained before. For the poorer countries of the region, the situation is dismal. It would seem that their development will now depend financially on the North, at the expense of their political independence. Indeed, the United States used aid to apply pressure on countries such as Syria and Egypt to join the coalition. It now seems unlikely that even these countries will be much richer after their pay-off.

The United States may have wiped US$7 billion off Egypt's military debt, but Cairo still has US$35 billion in debt arrears. Added to a loss of US$7 billion a year as a result of the economic disruption caused by the war, the prospect of real development slides away. Syria is to receive US$2 billion in aid from Saudi Arabia, and its funds were unblocked by the European Community. Yet the pressure to keep on arming is high in the region due to Israel's intransigence, and there are rumours of a US$20 billion Syrian arms deal with the Soviet Union.

Other countries such as Jordan and Yemen, which have failed to toe the line, are in even deeper trouble. Yemen, the poorest country in the Middle East, a 'Least Developed Country' according to the UN classification, has lost US$1.7 billion so far (20 per cent of its GNP), mostly as a result of the expulsion of its 800,000 migrant labourers from Saudi Arabia. Additionally, the United States has cut its planned development aid from US$22 million to US$2.9 million. Jordan has suffered losses of up to US$10 billion through costs and loss of savings and investments. Saudi, Kuwaiti and Iraqi aid has been lost, and the US aid programme (US$85 million annually) is being reviewed. Unemployment is rife, and the United Nations Children's Fund has reported whole sectors of the Jordanian population slipping into poverty. A new phenomenon, 'undevelopment', seems to be sweeping the region, like a fantastic time machine working only in reverse. The destruction of the developing, technology-oriented state of Iraq, cast back into pre-industrial times, seems to have triggered a chain reaction in the neighbouring countries.

Iraq's development was destroyed with refined perversity, in a war aimed at irreparably maiming its development achievements in the long term. Its energy production capacities were nearly wiped out, paralysing all basic services and preventing crops from being harvested. Communication systems were wrecked, rendering any sort of disease monitoring impossible. Its agricultural and medical industries were nearly obliterated, forcing it to rely on future imports. Civil war is shattering the country in the north and the south at the cost of thousands of deaths. Iraq was, three months back, a developing nation capable of challenging the interests of the mighty North. And that was the mistake of its foolish ruler, a mistake big enough to make the world's rulers decide to send Iraq back to the 'Least Developed' countries.

What has happened to Iraq, and is in the process of happening to many other Arab countries, is not incidental. It coincides with the demise of the Soviet Union and the emergence of the so-called New World Order, enforced by the United States and sanctioned by the UN; an order in which the poor nations must obey or be pushed back into underdevelopment. This new order is bold and shameless; US officials have already declared that under article 51 of the UN Charter, which restricts the use of force to self-defence against armed attack, the United States will use armed force to 'defend its interests'. The Gulf War has violently ended one global conflict only to usher in a new one. It has shown that the fight for the domination of the South and its resources is no longer between the West and the East, but between the powerful in the North and the people of the South. It has left little scope for development.

Conclusion

John Gittings

This book arose out of concern over media manipulation and distortion of truth during the Gulf War, and the way Middle Eastern opinion was excluded from the debate. Now the war has 'ended', does the public have a clearer perception of what happened and are we listening more to those people most closely affected?

There is some reason for optimism that, given a fair chance, public opinion will identify and defend positions which are both moral and effective. When journalists and photographers were at last able to shake off their military minders during the allied advance on Kuwait, their reports of the allied 'turkey shoot' on the road to Mitla did put a powerful brake on further mass slaughter.

When the pictures of death and degradation among Kurdish refugees could be seen nightly, the Western allies were shamed into mounting a more adequate relief effort. There were still gross distortions. The Kurdish refugees who headed for Turkey — a Western ally — received far more publicity than the much greater numbers who were allowed to enter neutral Iran. The reason for their exceptional suffering on the mountainsides (Turkey's refusal to allow them entry) was obscured by the British and US plan to shift them back to 'safe havens' in northern Iraq. This plan then became very largely the Kurdish story. Grotesque insults to humanity were reported with staggering matter-of-factness. On 23 April Western media calmly carried a statement by the White House spokesman Marlin Fitzwater that the death rate of Kurdish refugees along the Turkish-Iraqi border appeared to have 'stabilised' at roughly 510 deaths a day — 'down by half' from a previous daily total of one thousand.

Yet overall the media were able to inform public opinion and reflect its outrage. This was admittedly more marked in Europe than in the United States, given its appetite for military triumph that Richard Falk has remarked in his essay earlier. The question he poses is whether the

Conclusion

people, if informed and free, will restrain the militarism of the state. Perhaps the real problem is that it is unlikely that we will ever be fully informed and wholly free. Yet that must remain our purpose. There are still grounds for hope that some of the more glaring lessons of this war and its aftermath will have been registered in our collective memories. Post-war evidence has provided greater detail on how, when Saddam Hussein belatedly conceded defeat and through Soviet mediation announced publicly his willingness to leave Kuwait, the United States insisted on launching its ground offensive. It was the view of President Gorbachev that 'the differences between the formula to which Iraq had agreed and the proposals from a number of other countries were not so great that they could not be worked out in the Security Council in one or two days'.[1] Evidence has also emerged of the French initiative on the eve of the expiry of the 15 January ultimatum. Like the Soviet and other European initiatives, this was regarded as meddlesome interference by Washington and London.

The shabby tale of the West's encouragement to the Iraqi people to rise up against Saddam came soon enough after the war to tarnish the mood of triumphalism (particularly outside the United States). Whether or not specific incitement occurred — at least two presidential directives for covert support appear to have been issued — is less important than President Bush's repeated insistence that there would only be lasting peace if 'that man' were removed.

Hopes have been expressed that out of the evil of this war may come a better prospect of effective international peace-keeping action in the future. This is highly dubious, especially if coupled with the argument that the allies should have intervened militarily to assist the Kurds and the Shi'as. Such action would have had even less to do with the United Nations than the war itself. The UN as an independent body, and particularly its organisation in the person of the secretary-general, emerged from the war with diminished reputation. The allied 'save havens' in northern Iraq were set up without regard to an agreement signed on the same day in Baghdad between Iraq and the UN.

At best it might be said that the hijacking of the UN by the five permanent members of its Security Council (or by three of them with the reluctant consent of the other two) will now provoke more critical thought about the necessity for the Council's structural reform and enlargement. A proposal on these lines was jointly produced in April by the Stockholm Initiative on Global Security and Government which included members of the Palme, Brandt, Brundtland and South Commissions.

It is suggested that the Gulf War and the Kurdish tragedy will have the effect of modifying previous international respect for what some regard as the 'narrow' principle of non-interference in internal affairs. A broader view of the essential interdependence of nation states in the modern age may well be desirable. But it will only begin to have a genuine character if it addresses all cases of internal oppression with equal energy — East Timor as well as Kuwait, the West Bank as well as Kurdistan. And the strongest test of any nascent internationalism will be its ability to deal with the hitherto unstoppable traffic in lethal arms to the Third World.

The Palestine question has indeed received new attention since the end of the Gulf War in a form of retrospective 'linkage'. (Hundreds of thousands of lives might have been saved if such linkage had been allowed to provide Saddam Hussein with a face-saving way out of his folly.) As Alain Gresh argues, it may now be in the US interest to seek to promote a viable Palestinian settlement. But in any event there was no sign during Secretary of State James Baker's three missions in March-June of any US intention to apply real pressure upon Israel — even though one tenth of the effort which was applied to the war could be sufficient.

Yet the traumatic events of the war have begun to create a different sort of linkage, as Marion Farouk-Sluglett and Peter Sluglett also argue: that there will be no lasting peace in the Middle East until the governments of the region are 'fully accountable to their people'. Pressure for democracy in Kuwait, and for a stop to the human rights abuses which its restored rulers at first condoned, also establishes a new marker in the region. It will no longer be quite so easy for the West to regard the Gulf monarchies so indulgently. Yezid Sayigh writes about the structural weaknesses of this autocratic Arab state system which became pervasive after the Iraq-Iran war and the decline in oil revenues. These may be temporarily shored up by new security structures such as the 'six-plus-two' pact between the Gulf Co-operation Council, Egypt and Syria, signed after the Gulf War, which Youssef Choueiri describes. But there can be no long-term stability in an arrangement which rewards two coalition partners — including one headed by a ruler, President Assad of Syria, almost as monstrous as Saddam Hussein — with a special role, while marginalising the other regional power Iran.

What do the millions of Middle East citizens (and the stateless too) who do not have a share of their repressive state structures think of the outcome of the war? The 'deep hatred and anger' which our Jordanian contributor Fadia Faqir describes has gone underground. When even the post-war views of Arab governments are only skimpily reported, we cannot expect to understand the traumatised feelings of so many of their subjects. There is a Western assumption that they have been chastened — just as the PLO is presented as chagrined by its mistaken policy of 'support for Saddam', though Abbas Shiblak puts this in a more rational perspective, showing how the PLO has always been the victim of deliberate misunderstanding. To the extent that such is now the mood, it would be historically unsafe to assume that it will persist for longer than the next set of food riots or the next external conflict. If linkage with democracy is one tendency, then an opposite linkage with resurgent fundamentalism (as Haleh Afshar strongly argues) must also be considered.

At this point it becomes imperative to consider the economic prospects for the region which will have a powerful influence upon its available political options. In the final paper of this book, Rami Zreik shows that Arab 'wealth' has barely reduced its dependence upon imported technologies, while indigenous skills (including particularly those of the Palestinian diaspora) have been further eroded by the scattering effect of the war. What then are the prospects for political stability, far less for political progress, in a new climate of xenophobic suspicions and war-induced 'undevelopment'?

This question prompts the essential reminder that poverty and deprivation should have been targets for war long before Saddam Hussein. The problem of famine and refugees, exacerbated by war, is not confined to Kurdistan. In the spring of 1991 Oxfam calculated that some 50 million people were at grave risk in an arc stretching from the Horn of Africa to the Afghan border. Just as the Gulf crisis outlasts the Gulf War, so the conflict between North and South subsumes those within the Third World.

Has the war then taught us a lesson for the future? As an object lesson in devastation, it may compel some pause before any comparable action is undertaken again. The environmental effects described by Fred Pearce are horrifying but could have been much worse. Surely it will not be so easy again to brush aside warnings of destruction such as the firing of the oil wells — or to ignore the damage (including part of the infamous 'oil slick') inflicted by the allied side. We must also fervently hope that in any future conflict the destruction of a country's economic infrastructure will not be so blithely accepted.

The horrifying picture conveyed by Tim Niblock of damage to Iraq, ranging from destruction of the main seed warehouses to the wrecking of most water pumping systems, should be as vivid as the plight of the Kurds. No wonder that in a shattered nation only the brutality of Saddam's machine survives. If the Middle East as a whole is not to lapse into even more mutual xenophobia, then there is a still greater need for regional unity. But this cannot be based upon old myths, taboos and false heroes, as Khalil Hindi argues here. The Arab intelligentsia must detach itself from the state. The state itself must adopt modern systems of thought and government.

We return in conclusion to the twin themes of just treatment by the outside world and proper democracy within the region. Any world order tried out in the Middle East which lacks these two ingredients is the old one, not the new.

Notes
1. Soviet envoy Yevgeny Primakov in *Time*, 11 March 1991

Chronology of the Gulf War

JULY 1990
16th Tariq Aziz, foreign minister of Iraq, accuses Kuwait and the United Arab Emirates of 'direct aggression' against Iraq, by encroachment on Iraqi territory and excessive oil production.
18th Iraqi President Saddam Hussein accuses Kuwait of stealing crude oil worth US$2.4 billion from inside Iraqi territory and repeats Iraq's claim to oil in the disputed border region.
19th Kuwait asks Arab League to arbitrate the border dispute.
22nd Nato sources in Kuwait report 30,000 Iraqi troops, plus tanks, moving towards the Kuwaiti border.
23rd Saudi Arabia puts its forces on alert.
24th Opec negotiators hold an emergency meeting in Geneva and agree new oil production levels.
25th US ambassador to Iraq, April Glaspie, tells Saddam Hussein: 'We have no opinion on Arab-Arab conflicts, like your border disagreement with Kuwait. This issue is not associated with America.'
26th Kuwait and the UAE agree to abide by the new Opec production and export levels.
31st Iraqi troops on the Kuwaiti border now thought to number 100,000.

AUGUST 1990
2nd Iraq invades Kuwait. The whole country is quickly seized; the Emir and family flee to Saudi Arabia. The UN Security Council meets in emergency session and votes 14-0 for Resolution 660 which condemns the invasion, calls for a ceasefire and demands an Iraqi withdrawal. US President Bush and British Prime Minister Thatcher call the invasion 'naked aggression'.
3rd Iraqi army pushes south towards Saudi Arabia. Bush warns Iraq

	not to invade Saudi. The US and Soviet foreign ministers make a joint statement condemning the invasion.
6th	King Fahd invites friendly forces into Saudi Arabia. United States sends a squadron of F-15 fighters and the 82nd Airborne Division. Iraqi troops begin rounding up British and US citizens in Kuwait City. Saddam says the seizure of Kuwait is 'irreversible'. UN votes 13-0 for comprehensive sanctions against Iraq.
8th	Bush announces that US troops are being sent to the Gulf. Britain sends air and naval units to Saudi.
9th	UN Security Council says Kuwait's annexation by Iraq is null and void, voting 15-0.
10th	Iraq orders the closure of all foreign embassies in Kuwait and calls for 'holy war' against the United States and Israel. Arab League votes 12-3 to send a peacekeeping force to Saudi Arabia.
12th	Saddam sets terms for a settlement: Israel must leave the occupied territories, sanctions against Iraq must end and an Arab peacekeeping force must replace US forces.
13th	Jordan's King Hussein says the United States is creating an 'explosive' situation.
14th	Saddam asks for a 'full peace' with Iran in return for territory taken by Iraq during the war, and an exchange of prisoners.
16th	Saddam threatens to intern 5,000 Britons and 2,000 Americans in Kuwait City. They are ordered to assemble at two hotels.
18th	UN Security Council adopts Resolution 664 demanding that foreigners be allowed to leave Kuwait and Iraq.
21st	Iraqi soldiers start rounding up westerners from their homes. Tariq Aziz offers the West 'talks without preconditions'. The United States says Iraq must abide by Resolution 660.
23rd	Saddam appears on TV with British hostages.
25th	Security Council adopts Resolution 665 authorising all necessary measures to enforce the economic embargo. Iraq declares Kuwait its 19th province.

SEPTEMBER 1990

10th	Helsinki meeting of Bush and Soviet President Gorbachev: they warn Saddam of 'additional measures' if he does not withdraw from Kuwait. Iraq and Iran agree to resume full diplomatic relations.
12th	Iranian Ayatollah Ali Khamenei calls for holy war against the United States.
13th	UN Resolution 666 passed, determining procedure to meet humanitarian food needs in Iraq and Kuwait.

16th UN Resolution 667 passed, condemning the violation of diplomatic premises in Kuwait.
25th UN Resolution 670 passed, imposing an air embargo on Iraq and Kuwait.

OCTOBER 1990
5th Gorbachev sends a special envoy, Yevgeny Primakov, to Baghdad, but talks achieve nothing.
21st Former British prime minister Edward Heath meets Saddam, secures release of 33 hostages.
23rd Saudi Arabia ejects 350,000 Yemenis from the country.
26th United States said to be planning to double its deployment of troops by the year's end.
29th UN Resolution 674 passed, demanding an end to hostage-taking. UN invites claims against Iraq for financial losses to other countries and says Iraqi 'war crimes' must be monitored.

NOVEMBER 1990
2nd US mid-term elections.
3rd Iraq says all hostages could go if enough of the major powers make a declaration against the use of force. US Secretary of State James Baker departs on a seven-day tour of Bahrain, Saudi Arabia, Egypt, Turkey, the Soviet Union, Britain and France.
6th Saddam orders release of 106 hostages, mostly Japanese. Chinese foreign minister begins tour of Egypt, Saudi Arabia, Jordan and Iraq.
7th Saddam releases 120 hostages, mainly German.
8th Having passed the mid-term elections, the Bush administration now announces its intention to double its troop deployment by Christmas. Iraq's chief of staff is sacked and replaced. Former West German chancellor, Willy Brandt, returns home with 179 hostages following visit to Iraq.
14th Jordanian efforts to convene an Arab summit collapse. Iran's foreign minister begins a two-day visit to Baghdad.
18th Iraq says foreigners can leave in batches between Christmas Day and March 1991.
19th Iraq announces that 250,000 more troops will go to Kuwait.
23rd Bush meets Syrian President Assad in Geneva.
26th Gorbachev tells Tariq Aziz in Moscow to withdraw from Kuwait and release all hostages.
27th Saudi foreign minister visits Moscow and promises US$4 billion in loans to the Soviet Union. British Labour member of

	parliament, Tony Benn, visits Baghdad.
28th	Britain resumes full diplomatic relations with Syria.
29th	UN Security Council passes Resolution 678, authorising 'all necessary means' to be used against Iraq if it does not withdraw from Kuwait by 15 January 1991. China abstains.
30th	Iraq rejects 678 as illegal and invalid. Bush invites Aziz for talks in Washington and offers to send James Baker to Baghdad, at any time before 15 January. The five permanent members of the Security Council say Iraq will not be attacked if it withdraws.

DECEMBER 1990

1st	Iraq accepts the offer of talks, saying that the Arab-Israeli problem must be prominent in any discussions.
2nd	Saddam tells French TV there is a 50-50 chance of war.
3rd	King Hussein meets Saddam and Yasser Arafat in Baghdad.
5th	James Baker tells the Senate foreign relations committee to prepare for the possible early use of force following 15 January.
6th	Baker hints at an international peace conference on the Middle East, including the Arab-Israeli problem, but only at what he calls 'the appropriate time'. Iraq ends its 'human shield' policy of holding hostages at important target sites and says all foreign nationals can leave in time for Christmas.
9th	King Hussein calls for a Middle East peace conference. The United States says Iraq's offer to receive Baker on 12 January, three days before the deadline, shows that it is 'not serious' about the talks. He insists on a visit before 3 January.
10th	Israeli Prime Minister Yitzhak Shamir visits Washington. Nearly 800 British begin arriving home.
12th	Saddam sacks and replaces his defence minister.
14th	Bush says the high-level meetings he proposed are now 'on hold' until Saddam agrees to see Baker before 3 January.
15th	Tariq Aziz cancels a plan to fly to Washington on 17 December.
17th	Baker warns Nato foreign ministers that Saddam may try to undermine the coalition by offering a partial withdrawal from Kuwait. This becomes known as 'the nightmare scenario'.
20th	Turkey asks for Nato forces to defend itself from Iraq.
23rd	US Defence Secretary Dick Cheney warns that the United States has a 'full spectrum' of weapons available for use against Iraq, including nuclear weapons (700 when deployment is complete, according to the British-American Security Information Council).

Chronology of the Gulf War

JANUARY 1991

4th Bush offers a Baker-Aziz meeting in Geneva on 7, 8, or 9 January.

5th Iraq agrees to meet James Baker in Geneva on 9 January. EC foreign ministers say they will meet Aziz afterwards.

7th Baker in London for talks with British Foreign Secretary Douglas Hurd, then similar talks in Luxemburg, Paris, Bonn and Milan.

9th Baker meets Tariq Aziz in Geneva. All hopes for peace are staked on the outcome. Talks last all day, raising expectations, but end with the two sides far apart. The United States refuses to accept any 'linkage' between the Kuwait crisis and the Palestinian question. Aziz refuses to accept a letter from Bush to Saddam, calling it 'insulting'.

11th UN Secretary-General Pérez de Cuéllar meets President Mitterrand of France and later EC foreign ministers in a last peace effort.

13th Pérez de Cuéllar meets Saddam in Baghdad but makes no apparent progress.

15th UN deadline for Iraqi withdrawal expires.

16th The war begins between six and seven pm, US East Coast time (the early morning of the 17th in the Gulf). US and British planes begin bombing strategic targets in Baghdad and elsewhere in Iraq. Bush's spokesman calls it 'the operation to liberate Kuwait', to be known as Operation Desert Storm. First priority targets are air defences, command and control systems, Scud missile sites, airbases, and nuclear and chemical facilities. CNN reporters immediately begin transmitting live reports from a Baghdad hotel room. Pérez de Cuéllar was not informed before the start of hostilities. Israel declares state of emergency and tells civilians to stay at home.

17th First eight Scud missiles launched from Iraq against Israel: no casualties. The West urges Israel not to retaliate; Israel reserves the right to retaliation if chemical weapons are used. White House says there will be no pause for diplomacy. Saddam says he will liberate all Palestine, Lebanon and the Golan Heights. Anti-US demonstrations in Yemen, Sudan, Algeria, Morocco, Mauritania, Pakistan and Bangladesh.

18th Turkey gives the United States permission to fly bombing raids from its bases. US military shows videos of laser-guided weapons to demonstrate their accuracy. Electricity and telephones are cut off in Baghdad.

20th Iraqi TV shows pictures of seven captured allied pilots. Iraq fires nine Scuds at Saudi Arabia. Allied bombing shifts to Republican Guard positions. The United States commits Patriot missiles to

	Israel. Soviet peace plan passed to Iraq's ambassador at the UN. Saddam calls for attacks on allied interests 'everywhere'.
21st	Iraq threatens to hold captured aircrew at target sites. Saddam rejects Soviet peace plan. United States and Britain reject any talk of a ceasefire.
22nd	Scud hits block of flats in Tel Aviv. Three die; around 70 injured. Iraqi opposition speaks of a failed army coup in Baghdad on 18 January.
24th	The United States announces further shift to attacking ground troop positions. Chief of Staff Colin Powell says of Iraq's army: 'First we are going to cut it off. Then we are going to kill it.' CNN shows bombed baby milk factory outside Baghdad; the United States says it was a chemical weapons facility.
25th	First naval engagments as Iraqi patrol boats sunk. First Iraqi air attack against allied ships launches Exocet but two planes shot down. Intelligence reports speak of a huge oil slick spreading south from Kuwait, said to be twice as large as the Exxon Valdez spill. Bush accuses Saddam of 'environmental terrorism'. TV news and the next day's papers show photographs of oil-covered cormorants, later known to have come from another, smaller spill.
27th	39 Iraqi planes have fled to Iran in last two days.
28th	Over 100 Iraqi planes now in Iran, where they will be detained for the duration of war.
29th	James Baker and Soviet foreign minister issue joint peace proposal which includes a promise to broker solution to Arab-Israeli problem. Bush administration taken by surprise and quickly tries to deny any 'linkage'.
30th	Iraqi troops occupy Khafji, a deserted coastal town inside Saudi Arabia. Jordan accuses allies of deliberately killing its citizens after four Jordanian truck drivers die on Baghdad-Amman highway.
31st	US and Saudi troops retake Khafji after 36 hours of fighting. Large pro-Saddam demonstration in Algiers. Kurdish opposition says up to 80,000 Iraqi troops have deserted to the northern mountains.

FEBRUARY 1991

4th	Iran's President Rafsanjani offers to mediate peace. Pérez de Cuéllar says: 'Something must be done to stop the war.'
6th	Iraq finally cuts diplomatic relations with the United States, Britain, and main allies. King Hussein openly sides with Saddam, saying it is 'a war against all Arabs and Muslims'.
10th	Gorbachev sends special envoy Primakov to Baghdad.

Chronology of the Gulf War

13th Two laser-guided bombs from US planes hit and completely destroy an underground bunker in the Amiriyah suburb of Baghdad. Hundreds of civilians sheltering inside are killed. TV pictures, for once uncensored by the Iraqis, cause worldwide concern. The United States sticks by its claim that the bunker was a genuine military target. Dick Cheney says Saddam may have deliberately encouraged civilians into a military facility.

15th Iraq launches a surprise peace offer. It will accept Resolution 660 and withdraw from Kuwait, which it no longer describes as its 19th province, but attaches a variety of conditions, such as suspension of all UN resolutions and Israel's withdrawal from the Occupied Territories. Bush quickly rejects the offer as 'a cruel hoax'; new British Prime Minister John Major calls it 'a bogus sham'. Bush adds: 'There is another way for the bloodshed to stop, and that is for the Iraqi people to take matters into their own hands, to force Saddam Hussein, the dictator, to step aside.'

16th Iraq begins discussions with Moscow, saying the issues attached to the offer are 'concerns' and 'not conditions'.

17th Coalition troops step up their probes across the border into Kuwait, skirmishing with Iraqi troops. Bush says 'no ceasefire, no pause', but is said to be staying his hand on the ground war while peace efforts by the Soviet Union continue: Tariq Aziz arrives in Moscow after travelling overland into Iran. The British Royal Air Force admits that a bomb landed off target in Fallujah, killing between 50 and 130 civilians.

19th New Soviet peace offer, dropping most of Iraq's previous conditions for withdrawal. Before Iraq has replied, Bush rejects it as 'well short of what is required'. Massive bombing raid on Baghdad.

21st Iraq accepts eight-point Soviet plan, involving a monitored withdrawal in 21 days, following a ceasefire. Large allied artillery assault across Kuwaiti border.

22nd Bush counters Soviet plan with his own ultimatum: Iraq must begin withdrawal by noon Gulf time the next day, and be out of Kuwait within a week, or face land war.

23rd Last ditch effort by the Soviets. UN Security Council meets for 20 minutes and adjourns. No sign of Iraqi withdrawal.

24th The land war begins with three broad swathes of allied forces driving into Kuwait and Iraq, encountering little resistance. 100,000 POWs are taken on the first day. Iraqi troops begin a final round of destruction in Kuwait City, destroying buildings, executing civilians and taking hostages.

25th Iraq orders all troops to leave Kuwait and agrees a new

26th three-point Soviet peace plan with no conditions attached. Bush's spokesman says: 'We don't think there's anything to respond to.'

26th Kuwait City is abandoned by Iraqi troops, who rush north towards the border and Basra. Bush says the attack will continue with 'undiminished intensity'. The retreating Iraqis are cluster-bomed as they clog highways north. Thousands die. Emir says there will be a period of martial law in liberated Kuwait and puts his son, Crown Prince Saad, in charge.

27th Bush calls a halt to hostilities from midnight. He demands that Iraq releases all PoWs and third country nationals, and all Kuwaiti detainees; that it complies with all relevant UN resolutions; and that it accept responsibility for paying compensation for damage and injuries. King Fahd says he will drop demands for reparations if Saddam is overthrown.

28th Iraq accepts all 12 UN resolutions. John Major calls on the people of Iraq to overthrow their 'pariah' president.

MARCH 1991

1st Basra reported in a state of anarchy, with anti-Saddam troops and demonstrators in the streets. Kurdish guerrillas reported on the move. Some 950 Kuwaiti oil wells are ablaze. Pérez de Cuéllar says sanctions against Iraq should not be maintained if the object is to overthrow the regime.

2nd Rebellion begins in Basra. UN adopts resolution enshrining Bush's ceasefire demands.

3rd Rebels in southern Iraq, loyal to exiled Shia cleric, Ayatollah Bakr al-Hakim, ask US forces for help in rebellion. Refugees from Iraq speak of widespread fighting in southern towns and say Basra is in rebel hands. Iraqi military leaders meet allied commanders near Safwan and agree to ceasefire terms.

4th Kurdish guerrillas seize Sulaymaniyah. Republican Guard begins push to retake Basra. Crown Prince Saad al-Sabah returns to Kuwait to enforce martial law.

5th Crown Prince imposes 10pm to 4am curfew. Reports of Kuwaitis harassing Palestinians. Kurds claim to have taken Irbil, while Shias claim to hold holy cities of Najaf and Karaba, and ten other towns. Fighting for Basra intensifies. Iraq says it has released all POWs and sends deputy prime minister to Tehran to offer power-sharing to Shias. Ayatollah al-Hakim refuses to meet him. James Baker begins week-long Middle East tour.

6th Republican Guard gaining upper hand in Basra. Saddam appoints new interior minister, his cousin Ali Hassan Majid, who was in charge of Kurdistan during 1988 gas attacks. Gulf states, Egypt

and Syria announce new security arrangement under which the latter two will guarantee military security for the others in return for freer trade.
10th Bush says PLO has 'lost credibility' on eve of Baker visit to Israel. Republican Guard, now mostly in control of Basra, storms Karbala.
11th Representatives of all Iraqi opposition groups meet in Beirut.
12th Syria releases hundreds of Palestinian prisoners.
13th Bush freezes arms sales to Middle East.
14th Emir returns to Kuwait. According to later reports, after successes in north-east, Kurds begin uprising in 12 towns which are taken by nightfall. Saddam's Kurdish regiments, the Jash, defect to the rebels and turn on regular troops, many of whom surrender.
17th The United States says it will enforce ceasefire terms preventing Iraq's use of aircraft but will not otherwise intervene in Iraq's internal affairs. The United States admits only around 300,000 Iraqi troops were in the battle zone when war began, not 500,000 as repeatedly claimed.
20th Kurdish rebels capture oil city of Kirkuk. The United States shoots down an Iraqi plane.
21st Saddam appears on TV with captured Shia cleric, outraging Shias. His government declares a state of emergency in Baghdad to stop rebellion spreading. US-based Middle East Watch says 2,000 foreign nationals, including Palestinians, are being detained and tortured in Kuwait.
22nd The United States shoots down second plane.
23rd Saddam reshuffles leadership. Tariq Aziz becomes deputy prime minister.
24th Kurds in control of most of Iraqi Kurdistan. Kurdish leader Masoud Barzani calls on all Iraqi opposition to set up a provisional government there. Government troops mass south of Kirkuk.
25th Iraqi aircraft and helicopters raid Kirkuk, Dohuk, Kifri and Kalar in northern Iraq. Kirkuk cut off from rest of region by government troops. Exodus of civilians begins. Kuwait says it will try 700 Palestinians for 'war crimes'.
26th The United States says it will not shoot down Iraqi helicopters. Al-Samawah, last town held by Shia rebels, falls to government. General Schwarzkopf says he wanted to 'annihilate' the Iraqi army but Bush stopped him short.
28th Iraqi government retakes Kirkuk after massive bombardment. Italian foreign minister calls on European governments to aid

Saddam's opponents. Refugees from southern Iraq speak of mass civilian executions in the towns.

31st   Rebellion in northern Iraq beaten back, with guerrillas unable to counter tanks, artillery and helicopter gunships. Baghdad claims control of Irbil and Dohuk. Thousands of refugees stream towards the borders. Over 50,000 refugees already in Iran, showing signs of chemical weapon attacks. Iraq accuses Iran of 'flagrant and gross interference' in its internal affairs. Arab League meeting finishes without mention of Iraq.

APRIL 1991

1st   Zakho, last important town held by Kurds, falls to government troops. Barzani appeals to West for tents, food, medicine and a UN initiative, as Kurdish towns empty and civilians flee into mountains.

2nd   Turkey says more than 200,000 refugees are in danger of dying on its border with Iraq. The Kurds say two million are on the move. Bush, on holiday, says: 'I'd rather not discuss it right now.' State Department spokeswoman Margaret Tutwiler says the United States 'never, ever stated as either a military or a political goal of the coalition, or the international community, the removal of Saddam Hussein.'

3rd   Turkey closes its borders to refugees. UN Security Council passes resolution setting terms for ending the war. Iraq must accept destruction of its chemical, biological and ballistic weapons; agree not to acquire or develop nuclear weapons; and accept a boundary with Kuwait demarcated by the Secretary-General of the UN, with UN observers placed along it.

4th   Turkey says 100,000 refugees are within its borders and half a million waiting for entry. Refugees are dying from exposure and exhaustion, from landmines, and from attacks by Iraqi helicopters, artillery and mortars. John Major pledges £21 million humanitarian aid but says: 'I do not recall asking the Kurds to mount this particular insurrection.'

5th   Nato accuses Iraqi government of 'massive human rights violations' against Kurds. Bush gives US$10 million aid and says US planes will commence aid drops.

7th   Iran closes its border after allowing 700,000 refugees in.

8th   John Major urges establishment of an 'enclave' (later altered to a 'safe haven') within northern Iraq, overseen by UN and protected by military force, to which refugees could return. EC agrees US$105 million aid to Kurds. James Baker spends seven minutes at refugee station in Turkish mountains. Iran reopens borders.

Kuwaiti government promises elections in August or September 1992.

9th United States warns Iraq not to attack Kurds and threatens force if it does so. Area covered by warning is said to be north of 36th parallel — most of Iraqi Kurdistan. Kuwait proposes 'safe haven' for Shia refugees in UN-supervised demilitarised zone.

Arming Saddam: The supply of British military equipment to Iraq 1979-90

In July 1979 Saddam Hussein took over as president of Iraq, his predecessor having resigned for 'health reasons'. To remove any possible remaining opposition to himself, Saddam immediately had 21 senior Ba'ath Party officials and members of the Revolutionary Command Council executed.

On 17 September 1980, just over a year after becoming President, Saddam abrogated the Treaty of Algiers that he himself had helped to draw up. Five days later his armies crossed the border into Iran: eight years of armed conflict had begun. After one million people had died in this war[1] a United Nations-sponsored ceasefire came into effect on 20 August 1988. Saddam's war against Iraq's Kurdish population, which in 1988 had included the use of poison gas, continued.

The cost of the war with Iran had left Iraq heavily in debt. In July 1990 Iraq accused neighbouring Kuwait of breaking international agreements by producing too much oil, thus lowering the world price and Iraq's income. On 2 August 1990, after Kuwait had in fact agreed to cut its oil production, Saddam's forces once again invaded a neighbouring state. The president was later to claim that, as part of the old Ottoman province of Basra, Kuwait was an artificial creation and was truly a part of historic Iraq. On 6 August the UN Security Council instituted an arms embargo against Iraq as part of a series of sanctions imposed as a result of the invasion.

According to the Stockholm International Peace Research Institute (Sipri), 6.9 per cent of Iraq's gross domestic product was accounted for by military expenditure in 1979. By 1984 this had risen to 29.1 per cent, falling only slightly to 27.5 per cent in 1985, the last year for which Sipri has percentages.[2] This compares with about 5 per cent for the UK in this period; only Angola comes anywhere near the Iraqi figure, with a few other Middle Eastern countries over 20 per cent. In monetary terms the 1984 figure is equal to US$31,590 million at 1988 constant prices and the 1985 figure amounts to US$23,506 million. Thereafter the spending declines.

Part of this military expenditure was used to purchase arms from overseas. During the first half of the 1980s Iraq was the world's biggest importer of major weapons systems and it remained second, behind India, in 1986 and 1987. A report by Sipri in 1987 identified 26 countries which had supplied arms both to Iraq and to Iran. These countries were: Austria, Belgium, Brazil, Britain, Bulgaria, Chile, China, Czechoslovakia, East Germany, France, West Germany, Greece, Hungary, Italy, North Korea, the Netherlands, Pakistan, Poland, Portugal, South Africa, Spain, Sweden, Switzerland, the United States, the Soviet Union and Yugoslavia. In addition, 12 countries had supplied only Iran while four countries had sold only to Iraq — Egypt, Ethiopia, Jordan and the Philippines. Not all of these deals were done with the knowledge or support of the government of the country concerned.

The long list above, however, conceals the fact that just two countries supplied most of Saddam's arsenal. According to the Sipri Yearbook in 1989, equipment from the Soviet Union accounted for 47 per cent and France 28 per cent of Iraq's major weapons systems during the Iran-Iraq war. The Soviet supplies included tanks, artillery systems, helicopters and missiles as well as advanced MiG aircraft.[3] Mirage and Super Etendard aircraft and Exocet missiles as well as helicopters and missiles were sold by French companies.

In November 1980, however, the Soviet Union had stopped its arms supplies and these were not resumed until after the Israeli air raid on Iraq's nuclear reactor at Osirak in July 1981.[4] The Soviet embargo, although short, made Iraq look elsewhere for its weapons. It served also to boost Saddam's ambitions to build his own arms industry and thus lessen his dependence on outside military supplies. France had its own problem with Iraq — extracting payment for the weapons became difficult towards the end of the 1980s. Ironically, this problem was to have been solved on the day of the invasion of Kuwait when the French government was due to sign a credit deal with Iraq to cover the latter's massive debts to French arms companies.[5]

Compared with the Soviet Union and France, the UK's role in arming Iraq may seem small. But it was not insignificant and it illustrates dramatically both the changing nature of the arms trade and the difficulties inherent in trying to control it.

It was on 29 October 1985, in a written reply to a House of Commons question, that the then foreign secretary, Sir Geoffrey Howe, announced the policy that remained in effect until the invasion of Kuwait:

> The United Kingdom has been strictly impartial in the conflict between Iran and Iraq and has refused to allow the supply of lethal

defence equipment to either side. In order to reinforce our policy of doing everything possible to see this tragic conflict brought to the earliest possible end, we decided in December 1984 to apply thereafter, the following guidelines to all deliveries of defence equipment to Iran and Iraq:

    (i) We should maintain our consistent refusal to supply lethal equipment to either side;
    (ii) Subject to that overriding consideration, we should attempt to fulfil existing contracts and obligations;
    (iii) We should not, in future, approve orders for any defence equipment which, in our view, would significantly enhance the capability of either side to prolong or exacerbate the conflict;
    (iv) In line with this policy, we should continue to scrutinise rigorously all applications for export licences for the supply of defence equipment to Iran and Iraq.

One of the problems with this stance was the concept of 'lethal' as distinct from 'non-lethal' equipment. It can be argued that all equipment used by the armed forces contributes to their actual or potential lethality. This was admitted by Colin Chandler, then head of the Ministry of Defence's Defence Export Services Organisation. Speaking at the 1986 British Army Equipment Exhibition (BAEE), Mr Chandler (now Sir Colin) said: 'There is no such thing as a "non-lethal" weapon.'

Five months after the ceasefire in the war with Iran, the 'guidelines' were 'being kept under constant review in the light of the ceasefire and developments in the peace negotiations'.[6] Over a year later, however, the 'guidelines' were still British government policy.

This, then, was the officially stated UK policy on military exports to Iraq until the August 1990 UN embargo. The real interest however lies in seeing how this policy was interpreted. The British government does not publish a list of the licences issued for the export of military equipment nor will it answer questions in parliament about specific deals, as it claims such information is commercially confidential. The government has even refused to provide details of the annual value of arms sales to Iraq despite having given similar figures in respect of Malaysia.[7] The information as to how the government has acted with regard to military sales to Iraq has therefore had to be gleaned from reports in newspapers and military magazines and from parliamentary statements and is of necessity incomplete.

The trade in military equipment does not operate in isolation from other trade. Background information on the UK's general commercial relationship with Iraq during the late 1970s and 1980s is essential for an understanding of the military-related trade which took place in this period.

Just days before vice-president Saddam Hussein assumed the presidency of his country in July 1979, he received the then British foreign secretary, Lord Carrington, in Baghdad and agreed to lift Iraq's selective trade embargo against the UK. This embargo had been imposed in July 1978 after Britain had expelled 11 Iraqi diplomats following the murder in London of a former Iraqi prime minister. The lifting of the embargo heralded a 'new page' in Anglo-Iraqi relations, Lord Carrington said, and the UK would look favourably on an Iraqi request for an economic agreement to boost trade. Restoring trade with Iraq was seen as particularly important in view of the loss of Iranian markets after the fall of the Shah. One deal with Iraq that was said to be outstanding from before the embargo was for 'hundreds of millions of pounds' of Plessey's military electronics.[8]

In July 1981, 11 months into the war with Iran, Douglas Hurd, then a minister of state at the Foreign Office, visited Baghdad to celebrate the anniversary of the 1968 revolution which brought the Ba'athists to power. The *Guardian* talked of Mr Hurd acting as a 'high level salesman' and pointed out that Iraq's requirement for a comprehensive air defence system, for which British Aerospace was a contender, was a 'tantalising prospect'.[9] In the same month, and after a year of negotiation, Iraq and the UK signed an economic and technical co-operation agreement. The new warmth between Baghdad and London would assist exporters and the new trade secretary, John Biffen, was to make an official visit to Iraq in October 1981.[10] At the meeting in Baghdad from 3 to 7 October 1981 the UK-Iraq Joint Commission was set up. It was to meet annually to discuss trading relations between the two countries.[11]

By 1983, however, there were problems. Iraq's oil revenues had fallen while its war spending was increasing. In August of that year the Confederation of British Industry advised companies not already doing business in Iraq not to enter the market because of that country's deteriorating financial situation.[12] Help was soon at hand, however. The then prime minister, Margaret Thatcher, announced that the Export Credits Guarantee Department (ECGD) was extending a £250 million loan to Iraq. Additionally, cash contracts worth US$200 million that had already been signed would be converted into credit. In exchange £30 million owed by Iraq to British companies would be paid without delay.[13] Reports on the ministerial meetings mentioned above — which took place during the Iran-Iraq War — show that military projects were often discussed. The reports said that the projects could not be started until hostilities ended.

The ceasefire in the Iran-Iraq War was only days old when it was announced that Tony Newton, then trade and industry minister, would be leading the UK delegation to the annual UK-Iraq Joint Commission 'to help British companies to benefit from the trade opportunities' arising from that ceasefire. By continuing to provide credit to Iraq during the war, the UK had earned 'favoured nation' status from Saddam Hussein's government.[14] The Joint Commission met in Baghdad in November 1988 and the deal concluded by Mr Newton there allowed £340 million worth of export credit for 1989, nearly double the £175 million available in 1988.[15] These credit facilities were again underwritten by the ECGD.

Asked by a questioner in the House of Commons before the Baghdad meeting whether human rights violations, including the use of chemical weapons by the Iraqi government, would be taken into account when considering the credit provision, Alan Clark, then at the Department of Trade and Industry, said: 'The Government is concerned by the denial of human rights wherever this occurs, and has consistently made our views clear to the Iraqi government on this subject. We have also made clear to the Iraqi government our condemnation of the use of chemical weapons. We will continue to do so. At the same time, we should not lose sight of the importance of developing political and economic relations with Iraq and the provision of export credit is a major contribution to this.'[16] The huge increase in credit provision would appear to give some indication of the weight the UK government gave to human rights considerations and trade interests respectively.

By the autumn of 1989, UK-Iraq trade relations were not running so smoothly and a meeting of the Joint Commission scheduled for October had to be postponed. Although the detention of British nurse Daphne Parish and Observer journalist Farzad Bazoft by Iraq was partly to blame for this deterioration, the main problem was arrears in Iraqi payments estimated at just below £80 million.[17] Energy Secretary John Wakeham went to Baghdad for a three-day visit to try and improve matters[18] and in December, at a London meeting of the Joint Commission, new credit of £250 million was agreed for 1990. Concern about arrears was given as the reason for the sharp reduction from the 1989 level.[19]

An interesting debate in the House of Lords casts light on why the government was prepared to continue underwriting loans to Iraq despite the apparently high level of financial risk involved. Asked about the contradiction between expressions of disapproval of the country's human rights record and the credits granted, the then trade minister Lord Trefgarne replied that 'if we cut off our trading relations...we would lose many opportunities to convey our views on other matters.' He went on to say that trade sanctions had 'never ever worked' and to remind his listeners that 'Iraq is sitting on oil reserves second only to those of Saudi Arabia. Indeed, I think that that makes it the second largest possessor of oil reserves in the world.'[20]

It is in the context of this general courtship of Iraq, temporarily impoverished by the eight-year war with Iran, but potentially very wealthy, that the UK's military links must be placed. There was also the factor that distrust of Iran under the mullahs led many in government, commerce and the media to see Iraq as a necessary counterweight to its neighbour.

For most of the 1980s Iraq was a country at war. Even when the fighting stopped in 1988 there was no peace settlement with Iran; indeed, there was not to be one until after Saddam's forces had invaded another neighbour, Kuwait, in 1990. It was against this background of conflict that the UK government considered applications from British companies for licences to export militarily-useful equipment to Iraq. Extreme caution would therefore have been appropriate. But Iraq was seen as a counterweight to Iran's power in the region and as an oil-rich country which was becoming a major trading partner with the UK.

These divergent pressures led to apparently contradictory action by the British government. It allowed the export of military equipment which it categorised as non-lethal and invited Iraq to the 1986 BAEE. Whether or not the machine tool manufacturers were actually told to imply their machines were for civil use when applying for the licence, the Department of Trade and Industry does not appear to have investigated or taken action on reports that these machines and other equipment were being used for military purposes. On the other hand the UK appears to have played a leading role in controlling the export of chemicals that might be used in weapons and the Foreign Office did step in to prevent the development grant going to the LearFan factory.

Exporting military equipment to Iraq, however, was not something done by the UK alone. Indeed, as we have shown, the Soviet Union and France were Iraq's major suppliers. With regard to the sale of components and military technology, West Germany was probably most heavily implicated. The invasion of Kuwait alarmed people not only in the UK but around the world and has prompted fresh consideration of arms transfer issues. In many countries governments and opposition parties are looking at their arms export laws to see how they can be strengthened. Perhaps most significantly, the crisis in the Gulf prompted the former Soviet foreign minister, Eduard Shevardnadze, to suggest that his country draft new laws to control its arms exports. He also wrote to the UN secretary-general pressing for international action. He wanted particular attention paid to stopping the proliferation of missiles and missile technologies and making sure that arms reductions in one region do not result in military rivalries elsewhere. He urged restraint on the transfer of arms to areas of conflict. The former Soviet foreign minister also proposed the establishment of an arms trade register and that customs and law-enforcement agencies should co-operate to stop the illegal arms trade in the same way as is done with regard to drug-trafficking. The invasion of Kuwait has starkly illustrated the dangers of the indiscriminate trade in arms and indicate that the consideration of proposals such as Mr Shevardnadze's are long overdue.

Notes
1. *World Military and Social Expenditures* 1989
2. *Sipri Yearbook 1990*, Stockholm International Peace Research Institute
3. *Jane's Defence Weekly* 18 Aug 1990
4. *Financial Times* 11 Nov 1980, 6 July 1981
5. *Times* 4 Aug 1990
6. *Hansard* 18 Jan 1989
7. *Hansard* 18 Nov 1990
8. *Financial Times* 5 July 1979
9. *Guardian* 17 July 1981
10. *Financial Times* 25 July 1981
11. *DTI Information Service*
12. *Financial Times* 11 Aug 1983
13. *Financial Times* 7 Oct 1983, *Times* 7 Oct 1983
14. *Independent* 24 Aug 1988
15. *Financial Times* 8 Nov 1988
16. *Hansard* 4 Nov 1988
17. *Financial Times* 14 Oct 1989
18. *Financial Times* 16 Oct 1989
19. *Financial Times* 1 Dec 1989
20. *Hansard* 14 Dec 1989

Extract from *Arming Saddam: The Supply of British Military Equipment to Iraq 1979-1990*, available from Campaign Against Arms Trade, 11 Goodwin Street, London N4 3HQ, phone 071-281 0291. Written January 1991, minor revision March 1991.

The Trust for Research and Education on the Arms Trade (Treat) promotes research into the international arms trade and its effects and disseminates the results of such research.

The economic impact of the Gulf crisis on Third World countries

As development agencies, our main responsibility in relation to the Gulf crisis is to draw attention to its consequences for poor communities worldwide. We can draw on two sources of evidence:

- Our overseas partners' and workers' reports of immediate hardships for poor communities and for the development programmes we support.
- A study of the economic impact of the crisis, and responses to it, which we jointly commissioned from the Overseas Development Institute (ODI) in London.

Main findings

1. At least 40 low- and lower-middle income developing countries are now facing the equivalent of a natural disaster due to causes which were externally generally and beyond the control of domestic policy makers. While the immediate crisis is likely to be of short duration, in terms of oil prices, its impact exceeds one per cent of the countries' gross national product (GNP). Of these countries, 16 are suffering an impact of more than two per cent of GNP, including states as far from the Gulf as Jamaica and Portugal. Yemen has lost over ten per cent of GNP, Jordan over 25 per cent.

The ODI estimates the total direct cost to low-income countries as US$3.2 billion. When lower-middle income countries are added, the cost comes to US$12 billion.

The aid organisations warn that these figures are likely to be an underestimate for a variety of reasons. They only include direct economic losses, not secondary effects such as production bottlenecks, and exclude loss of exports and higher freight costs due to a period of higher oil prices. They use official figures for the lost remittances sent home by migrant workers in the Gulf, many of which did not go through official channels; and they assume low resettlement costs for returning migrants.

2. Fourteen of the 40 countries are low-income sub-Saharan African countries which were already struggling before the crisis broke. They include four countries for which aid organisations have made a Disasters Emergency Committee appeal because of famine: Ethiopia, Liberia, Sudan and Mozambique.

3. The cost of compensating these countries is manageable for the world community. The ODI's figure of US$12 billion is less than the debt-forgiveness already offered to Egypt alone. The cost of the war itself is estimated at around US$100 billion.

How the crisis hit the Third World

Between August 1990 and January 1991 the price of oil averaged US$30 a barrel, compared to US$15-20 before the crisis and US$17-20 since the war began. The cost of oil imports rose, as did transport and freight costs, and this had a knock-on effect on all prices. Fuel prices fell back only slowly and in some countries continued to rise after the war began.

Poor people in Third World countries bear the impact of higher prices disproportionately. Kerosene, for many their main cooking fuel, rose faster in price than petrol in many countries. Travel costs in major cities doubled to take about a quarter of a worker's monthly wage. In Uganda public transport was so severely curtailed that thousands more people had to walk miles to work or school. In Pakistan, fuel was rationed and petrol prices rose 40 per cent.

Development work was also affected. The cost of food airlifts to Sudan, for example, rose by 46 per cent.

Those developing countries who had large numbers of migrant workers in the Gulf suffered both a loss of remittances and the cost of accommodating large numbers of returnees.

Demand for developing countries' exports fell as higher oil prices slowed the world economy. The World Bank suggested these losses will amount to US$6 billion, or one per cent. Some countries lost export markets and service contracts in Iraq and Kuwait. Tourism has reduced.

Finally, some countries suffered a loss of aid. This is clear for countries near to the Gulf who did not actively support the coalition, such as Yemen. It is less clear whether the costs of war may reduce donors' aid budgets, or whether compensatory payments already made to countries such as Egypt may be diverted from existing aid budgets. For example, one third of the US$2 billion pledged by the EC to the Gulf Crisis Financial Coordination Group is to come from the EC budget, and the UK's contribution to this will come from the aid budget.

Case studies: low-income countries

YEMEN: The ODI estimates the cost of the crisis to Yemen as at least US$830 million — ten per cent of GNP and 75 per cent of its exports of goods and services. Yemen's own estimate is US$1.7 billion.

As a result of Yemen's neutral stance, Saudi Arabia revoked residence rights for Yemeni workers, provoking a mass exodus of around 800,000 by November 1990. These workers, 15 per cent of Yemen's labour force, used to remit US$400 million per year.

In January 1991, the United States was reported to have reduced its planned aid from US$22 million to US$2.9 million.

ETHIOPIA: The ODI estimates the cost of the crisis as over US$110 million, nearly two per cent of GNP. This shock coincides with severe famine and civil war. We fear the focus on the Gulf War may reduce the international response to the famine. In addition, the relief operation has become more costly.

SUDAN: The Gulf crisis, causing a 100 per cent increase in oil prices and a fall in remittances, has cost Sudan nearly US$400 million: 2.9 per cent of GNP. This compounds the problems of an economy already devastated by civil war, mismanagement, and natural disasters. Fuel shortages are delaying deliveries of agricultural inputs and the food aid which many parts of Sudan are now relying on.

Sudan is in arrears with the International Monetary Fund and both IMF and World Bank funds have been halted. Sudan's stance in the Gulf War meets with disapproval from most potential donors.

BANGLADESH: The ODI estimates a cost of US$240 million, 1.2 per cent of GNP. Since much of the cost is caused by lost remittances, estimated by the government as US$500 million a year, this is a conservative figure.

SRI LANKA: The ODI estimates a loss of US$265 million, 3.7 per cent of GNP; a third of that is from lost remittances. Civil war had already made the economic situation difficult.

INDIA: The ODI estimate is a cost of US$1.6 billion overall, but this is much more severe for the states of Kerala and Gujerat, who had 200,000 workers in the Gulf.

Case studies: lower-middle income countries

JORDAN: The most affected country, Jordan has lost US$1.8 billion, 25 per cent of GNP and 75 per cent of its exports of goods and services. The 300,000 workers who have returned represent a tenth of the labour force. Many are Palestinians, who may not be re-employed in the future.

Jordan has lost aid from Iraq, Kuwait and Saudi Arabia totalling US$200 million in the second half of 1990 alone. The US is reviewing its US$85 million a year aid programme.

Jordan was attempting to switch from Iraqi to Saudi Arabian oil supplies, in accordance with the embargo, when Saudi Arabia cut its supplies, forcing Jordan to introduce sweeping energy-saving measures and return to Iraqi imports. Recent reports, however, speak of all Iraqi supplies ceasing. In addition, Jordan lost export markets in Iraq and Saudi Arabia.

A December 1990 United Nations Children's Fund report said: 'Many families have slipped into poverty because their main breadwinner suddenly found himself unemployed due to the impact of the Gulf crisis.'

OCCUPIED TERRITORIES: Palestinians in the Territories have lost remittances, trade, and support from Gulf states, totalling US$366 million a year, according to the Geneva-based Welfare Association. The curfew imposed on them by Israel has cut 304,000 Palestinians off from their sources of income: the daily loss is estimated at US$5.2 million. Long-term development work is largely suspended.

International responses to date

The Gulf Crisis Financial Coordination Group has been pledged US$13.6 billion in aid for the most immediately affected countries; but this is narrowly focused, with US$10.5 billion going to Egypt, Turkey and Jordan.

The IMF has expanded its highly concessional Enhanced Structural Adjustment Facility (ESAF), but only five of the 18 severely affected low-income countries have ESAF programmes. New ones take time to negotiate because of the strong conditions attached.

The World Bank will speed up its projected disbursement, but the loans are heavily conditional, and new money will be needed.

Recommendations for international action

All UN member states affected by the crisis should get aid and/or debt relief, independent of their political stance, and on a criterion of greatest need. The conditions attached to loans should be reduced.

Contributions should be additional to existing or planned resources. The British and other governments should declare what contributions have been made from their aid budgets to the Gulf effort or to compensating developing countries for their losses.

The fact that so many countries affected fall into the low-income category suggests assistance should be at concessional rates. Those countries experiencing debt problems need concessional lending and/or debt reduction. Some countries need short term finance only; others require longer-term help. Those coping with large numbers of returnees need special help with resettlement and rehabilitation.

Mechanisms for assistance

- UN-backed sanctions and military action have brought harsh economic consequences to many developing countries. A political decision is needed to recognise these as costs of the UN action. Article 50 of the UN Charter, which allows compensation to countries disadvantaged as a result of Security Council decisions, should be implemented. This compensation could come either through a specific fund-raising exercise operated bilaterally, or by existing instruments of the UN system like the World Bank and IMF using their more concessional and less conditional channels.
- Some of the resources contributed through the Gulf Crisis Financial Coordination Group should be directed to a broader group of countries.
- The World Bank should contribute all this year's record 'net income' (profits) from IBRD lending either to IDA or to schemes to tackle the current crisis. Industrialised countries and major oil exporters should be asked to make additional IDA pledges.
- In October 1990 the IMF's managing director, Michel Camdessus, proposed a 'subsidy account' financed by those who benefitted from higher oil prices and by voluntary contributions. We urge returning to this proposal. For low-income countries, unused EDAF resources could be redeployed to subsidise lending under the non-conditional Compensatory and Contingency Financing Facility.

Source: Memorandum to the Foreign Affairs Select Committee, jointly submitted by Cafod, Christian Aid, CIIR, Oxfam, Save the Children Fund, and World Development Movement, March 1991.

The Palestinian memo to James Baker

The following is the full text of the memorandum presented by a group of Palestinian nationalists to US Secretary of State James Baker during their meeting in Jerusalem on 12 March 1991 at the home of US Consul Philip Wilcox:

The Honourable US Secretary of State James Baker
The US Consulate General
Jerusalem

In the aftermath of the Gulf War, neither regional nor global politics can afford procrastination or evasion. As Palestinians who have been made to endure prolonged occupation and dispossession, we are heartened by verbal commitments and statements of intent to solve the Palestine Question on the basis of the principle of land for peace and the implementation of all pertinent UN resolutions.

From our experience, however, resolve and application hold the fate of our whole nation in sway. We maintain that, in spite of the painful and traumatic experience of the Gulf War, the time has come for embarking on decisive and future-oriented action rather than indulging in recrimination and retrospection.

It has thus become imperative that the activation of the UN as the expression of the will of the international community be impartially maintained in the non-selective implementation of legality and the values of justice and moral politics.

If a new global vision is emerging, it must be solidly based on the objective will and consent of the international community and must protect the inviolable rights of peoples as enshrined in the UN Charter and all other international conventions and agreements.

Such a vision of justice, peace and stability cannot admit the subjective criteria of power, wealth, land acquisition, strength of arms, natural resources, ethnic origins, religious affiliation, cultural perspectives or national identity as factors in upholding rights and passing judgements.

Nor must such resolutions be held captive to the intransigence of the violator in relation to the victim or to the manipulation of the powerful to the weak. The will of the international community must be maintained as a firm and uniform reference for equitable arbitration not subject to selective alteration or deferment.

We, the Palestinians of the *intifada*, the portion of the Palestinian nation who bear the yoke of occupation rather than exile and dispersion, on the strength of our commitment to this new vision affirm the following:

1. The PLO is our sole legitimate leadership and interlocutors, embodying the national identity and expressing the will of the Palestinian people everywhere. As such, it is empowered to represent us in all political negotiations and endeavours, having overwhelming support of its constituency. The Palestinian people alone have the right to choose their leadership and will not tolerate any attempt at interference or control in this vital issue.

2. We confirm our commitment to the Palestinian peace initiative and political programme as articulated in the 19th PNC of November 1988, and maintain our resolve to pursue a just political settlement of the Palestinian-Israeli conflict on that basis. Our objective remains to establish the independent Palestinian state on the national soil of Palestine, next to the state of Israel and within the framework of the two-state solution.

3. Our adherence to the international legitimacy remains unwavering, and we uphold the rule of international law in accepting and supporting all UN resolutions pertaining to the Question of Palestine, and thus call for their immediate and full implementation.

4. The national rights of the Palestinian people must be recognised, safeguarded and upheld — foremost among which is our right to self-determination, freedom and statehood.

5. No state must be singled out for preferential treatment by the international community or considered above the norms and laws that govern the behaviour of or relations among nations. Thus Israel must not be allowed to continue pre-empting, rejecting or violating UN resolutions vis-à-vis the Palestinians, especially in the annexation of East Jerusalem, the establishment of settlements and the confiscation of land and resources.

Of particular relevance and urgency is the imperative necessity of applying the Fourth Geneva Conventions of 1949 to protect the defenceless and civilian Palestinian population from the brutality of the occupation, particularly in its persistent violations of our most basic human rights and all forms of collective punishments such as house demolitions, closure of universities and schools, curfews, military sieges, and economic strangulation.

6. The *de facto* sovereignty which Israel illegally practices over occupied Palestine must cease immediately, and a system of protection for Palestinians and accountability for Israel must be established and applied within the mandate of the UN with the Security Council exercising its right of enforcement.

7. The peace process must be advanced with the momentum generated by the will of the international community, and not made subject to Israeli concurrence and rejection.

8. The most suitable mechanism for advancing the peace process is the International Conference which is capable of producing concrete results. Any transitional steps or arrangements will have to be structured within a comprehensive, inter-connected and coherent plan with a specified time frame for implementation and leading to Palestinian statehood.

9. The peace process cannot be further undermined by Israel's policy of creating facts to alter the geopolitical, demographic, or social realities of our area. The political decapitation of the Palestinian people through the arrest and detention of our political activists and peace advocates must stop and the detainees released. The 'Iron Fist' policy and the escalation of all forms of repression and harassment not only create intolerable conditions for Palestinians but also generate feelings of hostility and bitterness which are capable of sabotaging the peace process.

10. Security for the whole region will be ensured only through a genuine and internationally-guaranteed peace, not through the acquisition of arms and territory or violence. Genuine peace and stability will result from addressing the central causes of conflicts in a serious and comprehensive manner, the Palestinian question being the key to regional stability. Only by solving the Palestinian-Israeli conflict can the Arab-Israeli conflict be solved in a durable and just manner.

11. The stability and prosperity of the region can be achieved through future co-operation based on mutuality, reciprocity and recognition and pursuit of joint interests and rights.

As Palestinians under occupation, we are able to transcend the inequities and oppression of the present and to project a future image of peace and stability. In doing so, we affirm our national rights, adhere to international legitimacy and envisage the prospects of a new world based on the politics of justice and morality.

East Jerusalem, 12 March 1991

Contributors

Haleh AFSHAR was born and raised in Iran. She has been living in exile in Britain since the revolution. She teaches politics and women's studies at the University of York.

Youssef CHOUEIRI was born in Lebanon, educated at the American University of Beirut and Cambridge. He is lecturer in modern Middle East history at the University of Exeter and author of *Arab History and the Nation State* and *Islamic Fundamentalism*.

Richard FALK is professor of international law at Princeton University. He has been a counsel before the International Court of Justice, acting director of the Centre for International Studies and a consultant to the US Senate foreign relations committee.

Fadia FAQIR is a Jordanian writer who lives in Britain. Her first novel *Nisanit* was published by Penguin (1987) and her second novel, *The Yarn Spinner*, is forthcoming.

Marion FAROUK-SLUGLETT is lecturer in politics at University College of Wales, Swansea, and co-author with Peter Sluglett of *Iraq Since 1958: From Revolution to Dictatorship*.

Michael GILSENAN is professor of contemporary Arab studies at Oxford University and the author of *Recognising Islam* (Tauris).

John GITTINGS is on the editorial staff of the *Guardian*, and is treasurer of the Gulf Conference Committee. He co-authored (with Noam Chomsky and Jonathan Steele) *Superpowers in Collision* (Penguin, 1984).

Alain GRESH writes for *Le Monde Diplomatique* and is co-author of *A to Z of the Middle East* (Zed).

Khalil HINDI has dual Palestinian and British nationality and teaches computing at University of Manchester Institute of Science and

141

Technology. He has written and lectured on Middle Eastern affairs and Palestinian issues.

Tim NIBLOCK is senior lecturer in Middle Eastern politics at Exeter University. His books include *Iraq the Contemporary State; State, Society and Economy in Saudi Arabia; Social and Economic Development in the Arab Gulf;* and *Class and Power in Sudan.*

Fred PEARCE is a freelance environmental writer who contributes regularly to the *Guardian* and *New Scientist.* He is author of *Turning Up the Heat* (Bodley Head, 1989).

Yezid SAYIGH, a Palestinian, is a research fellow at St Antony's College, Oxford, where he works on international relations and Third World security. His most recent publications are *Confronting the 1990s: Security and the Developing Countries* and *Arab Military Industry.*

Abbas SHIBLAK is a Palestinian writer and Middle Eastern analyst and author of *Lure of Zion: The Case of the Iraqi Jews.*

Peter SLUGLETT is lecturer in modern Middle Eastern history at Durham University and co-author with Marion Farouk-Sluglett of *Iraq Since 1958: From Revolution to Dictatorship.*

Rami ZREIK studied at the American University of Beirut before doing his doctorate in agriculture at Oxford. He has been involved with development work in Lebanon and Bahrain and has been CIIR's country representative in Yemen for the past year.